PAPER DREAMS

UNIVERSE BOOKS ◆ NEW YORK

PAPER DREAMS

WRITTEN & ILLUSTRATED BY

LORRAINE BODGER

Thanks and love to Delia Ephron
for indispensable help and counseling on PAPER DREAMS and
for work we've done together that prepared me to do a book on my own.

Published in the United States of America in 1977
by Universe Books
381 Park Avenue South
New York, N.Y. 10016

© Lorraine Bodger 1977

Library of Congress Catalog Card Number: 76-21221

Cloth edition: ISBN 0-87663-287-8
Paperback edition: ISBN 0-87663-964-3

Printed in the United States of America

Designed by Lorraine Bodger

CONTENTS

1. THE BEST OF EVERYTHING:
   PAPERCRAFT SUPPLIES & WHERE TO GET THEM 9

2. PLAIN & FANCY: MAKING PATTERNED PAPER 19

3. PAPER-CUTTING 26

4. FLOWERS 41

5. HANGING ORNAMENTS 55

6. PARTY DECORATIONS 67

7. BOOKS 82

8. MASKS, TOYS, & SILLY HATS 96

9. BOXES & BASKETS 108

10. NOTES, CARDS, & INVITATIONS 118

PAPER DREAMS

Papercraft is magic: By a kind of sleight of hand, and with little more than paper, scissors, and glue, you can produce an extraordinary array of wonders—books and birds, baskets and toys, flowers and cards. Papercraft does not require any special skills or special equipment. You don't even need much space. You can do a project that takes an hour or one that takes a day. Papercraft can be simple and satisfying or complex and challenging.

PAPER DREAMS is a collection of decorative paper projects, things to make for your home and family, for friends, for your personal use, and for pure pleasure. The projects are easy to understand and the results are delightful to look at. You'll have a magical time with papercraft—better than you ever dreamed.

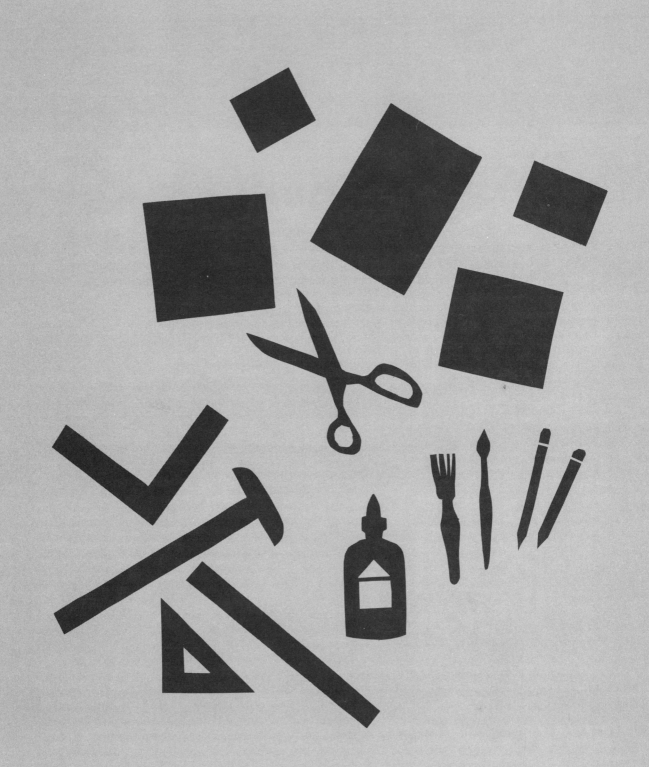

I. THE BEST OF EVERYTHING: PAPERCRAFT SUPPLIES & WHERE TO GET THEM

There's no question about it: You should have the best of everything, and best means right—the right paper, the right scissors, the right glue. If you don't happen to know right from wrong now, you will by the time you finish reading this chapter. You'll know exactly what supplies to ask for and where to ask for them.

The first part of the chapter is a complete list of essential supplies with descriptions and illustrations of each. Next you'll find a rundown of the right stores to scout for these essentials. In case you are closer to a post office than a shopping center, I have listed mail-order houses that carry many of the materials you'll need. Finally, there is a Shopper's Guide that tells you item-by-item in alphabetical order where to find anything listed in the **Materials** section of each project.

So let's take it from the top with the most basic materials. Paper comes first.

PAPER

You don't need the fanciest and you won't want the rock bottom, so, in general, the middle ground is for us. The following catalogue will tell which papers are the right ones for the projects in this book.

Construction paper is the all-purpose craft paper that everyone grew up with. Remember those wonderfully promising packages of assorted colors you used to buy at the 5-and-10? Construction paper has grown up with you as you will find out in the projects you do. Look for it in packages of 12" x 18" sheets as well as the basic 9" x 12".

Tissue paper, the wispy paper that cushions your new dress when you take it home in a dress box, is frequently used for giftwrapping. Buy it in packages of brilliant, pastel, and variegated colors as well as white. Be on the lookout for art supply stores that sell individual sheets of many more fabulous colors.

Crepe paper is that crimped, stretchable paper you associate with streamer decorations for the Junior Prom. Leave the prom in the past and buy crepe paper only in the standard folded rolls.

Origami paper: the square paper customarily used in the Japanese art of paper folding. Keep the largest squares—9" x 9"—for folding, and the smallest—3" x 3"—for cutting decorations. The best thing about origami paper is that each package contains 30 or more sheets of paper in a rainbow of colors. Patterned origami paper is worth searching for; I actually own 3 packages of it—1 found in San Francisco, another in Seattle and the third discovered in New York.

Giftwrap paper: stripes, patterns, and solids in folded sheets or rolls. A careful search through a good import store may turn up some beautifully patterned Japanese giftwraps.

Bond paper: You know it as typing and Xerox papers. Look for white and pastel colors. Art supply stores carry white bond paper in pads—14" x 17" is a good, all-purpose size.

Newsprint paper is the kind of paper newspapers are printed on—but don't run out to retrieve yesterday's sports section from the trashcan. Buy a fresh, clean pad of white newsprint and, while you're at it, take a look at a similar paper called oatmeal paper. Newsprint is smooth while oatmeal paper has a texture something like—you guessed it—oatmeal.

Charcoal, pastel, and watercolor papers: The textures of these papers, ranging from fine-grained to pebbly, make them ideal for artists to draw and paint on. In fact, charcoal and pastel refer not to the color of the paper but to the sticks of chalk the artist uses. I love them for papercraft because of their unique colors—subtle neutrals, heathers, muted roses and blues, brilliant turquoise and emerald green.

Stationery and note papers: You probably have a drawerful of leftovers waiting to be used. If you don't, buy these new in pads and packages. Stay away from the kind with mushrooms and kittens in the corners.

Aurora paper is the brand name of the most common of the papers designated "colored 1 side only," meaning that the color is printed on 1 side and the other side is white. The colored side has a matte finish—not at all glossy but dull with a creamy texture.

Coloraid and Pantone are 2 other brands similar to Aurora.

Flint paper is also "colored 1 side only" but that side has a slick, shiny, high-gloss finish. Buy individual sheets or packages of assorted colors.

Metallic papers are "colored 1 side only" with gold, silver, or copper ink. Most are stiff, but metallic foil paper has the clingy, malleable quality of ordinary aluminum foil. Foil paper takes well to folding and pleating.

Rice paper: Hold a piece up to the light and you will see delicate little flakes and fibers that seem to be swimming in the paper. There are many different rice papers—some even have butterflies, leaves, and other exotica embedded in them—so I always have a hard time selecting which one I want. Checking the prices helps me choose because rice paper can run to a lot of money.

Tableau paper has the same fibrous quality as rice paper but it is much less expensive. Its main talent is absorbency, which makes it ideal for dip-in-dye decorating (see Chapter 2).

Tracing paper: You'll need a few small pieces for tracing patterns.

Kraft paper is good, brown wrapping paper. Cut up clean brown bags or buy this paper in rolls or folded sheets.

Shelf paper means ordinary, solid-color, 5-and-10-type shelf-lining paper that you buy in rolls. Shelf paper is not contact paper.

Bristol board is heavy paper like the kind that engraved invitations are printed on. It comes with either a smooth surface (called plate finish) or a slightly textured surface (called vellum finish). More important, it comes in 4 different weights (thicknesses)—1-, 2-, 3-, or 4-ply—so you can suit the weight to the purpose. One-ply is thin—like typing paper—and would be good for the endpapers of a book. Four-ply is heavy—like shirt cardboard—and would be good for making a box.

Poster board: If you've ever made a poster or even looked at one, you are probably acquainted with poster board. Poster board is the general alias of tag board, oaktag, and railroad board. Ask for any of these and you'll get large sheets of smooth, heavy, cardboard-like paper in a choice of colors.

Boards: There are many kinds of boards —chipboard, mat board, illustration board, etc., but the all-purpose board for us is Bainbridge board #172, single thick, H.P. (hot press) finish, available in 22" x 30" or 30" x 40" sheets. If your art supply dealer does not have this, she may be able to suggest an equivalent that you can try. Do not buy any double-thick boards for use in projects.

OTHER BASIC NECESSITIES

Now we move to the nuts and bolts of papercraft. NOTE: These basics will not be mentioned in the **Materials** listing in any project; I will assume that you have them on hand whenever you are working with paper.

Scissors: You will need 2 pairs—a small pair with straight, sharp-pointed blades (I prefer not to use the curved blade nail or cuticle type often recommended for decoupage work) and an ordinary, large household pair. If you can get a pair of scissors with extra-long blades, so much the better.

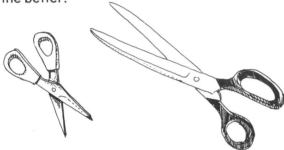

Glue: The only glue I ever use with paper is a standard white glue called Elmer's Glue-All, known from here on simply as glue. There are equivalents, like Sobo and Copydex, but I like Elmer's. Stay away from rubber cement, epoxy, mucilage, Elmer's School Glue, and other kinds of glue.

In this book, glue will be used in 2 ways: straight from the plastic bottle and slightly diluted. When a project calls for slightly diluted glue, pour some glue into a plastic container (like a clean margarine tub or a plastic cup), add a few drops of water, and mix well. The glue should be just a little thinner than full strength; it should not be runny or watery.

While glue is still wet, any excess that has been smeared around can be wiped off with a damp—not wet—paper towel. Don't worry too much about tiny smears because white glue dries clear.

Brushes: You will need 2 brushes for working with glue—1 small pointy brush and 1 large brush about ¾" to 1" wide.

Ruler and straight edge: An 18" metal ruler, which also functions as a straight edge for cutting with a mat knife or single-edge razor blade, is the best bet. However, a plastic or wooden ruler for measuring plus a metal straight edge for cutting is a perfectly adequate combination. (The straight edge can be a carpenter's metal square or triangle or even the bar of a metal T-square.)

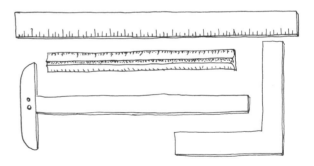

Single-edge razor blades: These are special blades that you buy in a hardware or art supply store. This is the only kind you should ever use for paperwork.

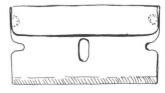

Actual size

Never use any kind of blade that goes in a shaving razor; it would be extremely dangerous.

Buy a dozen single-edge blades so you will have a good supply of new, sharp blades as you need them. Use only sharp blades; as soon as the blade begins to dull, turn it around and use the opposite corner. When that corner is no longer sharp, put a good-sized piece of tape around the whole blade and dispose of it safely. Take a new blade to continue the project. Keep single-edge blades far away from the reach of children.

If you have never used a single-edge razor blade, be sure to read the discussion of cutting on page 83.

X-acto knife: The X-acto knife consists of a narrow handle(#1 handle) and a thin, pointy blade (#11 blade) that screws tightly into the collar of the handle. Buy the blades in packets of 5; keep an extra packet on hand.

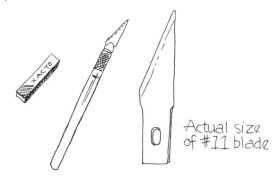

Actual size of #11 blade

Although you will not need this cutting tool for every project, it is indispensable for many of them. An X-acto knife is <u>not</u> used for heavy-duty work like cutting Bainbridge boards; it is used for delicate or hard-to-reach cuts that a scissor can't do.

Mat knife: There are 2 kinds of mat knives; one uses special blades of its own and the other uses single-edge razor blades (this kind is sometimes called a utility knife). A mat knife is used for general straight cutting, not for curves, and especially for heavy-duty cutting of boards and heavy papers. This kind of cutting is explained on page 83.

Again, you won't need a mat knife for every project, but it is essential for some.

Cutting surface: Chipboard, a heavy cardboard, serves this purpose well. You can also tear off the heavy backing-cardboard from a pad of drawing paper and use it for a cutting board. Never cut on a bare table and don't try to use shirt cardboard or corrugated cardboard as a cutting surface.

Pencils and erasers

Paper clips, clothespins, bulldog (or letter) clips: Keep a few of each on hand for holding paper in position while glue is drying.

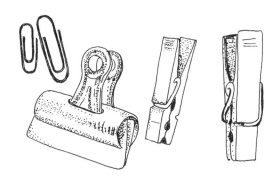

SPECIAL MATERIALS

Some projects call for materials in addition to the basic necessities. Check each project before you begin, to see if there is any special item you will need. The following list of equipment and decorative materials gives you a general idea of what you can be collecting for future use.

right-angle triangle, protractor, compass
paper punch
pipe cleaners, spools of wire and wire cutters
large needle and heavy-duty thread
string and cord (cotton string, Knit-Cro-Sheen, Speed-Cro-Sheen, pearl cotton, macramé cord)
scraps of ribbon and fabric
sequins, spangles, rhinestones, beads
stamp pads
toothbrush
paints (concentrated watercolors like Luma and Dr. Martin's brands, acrylics, oils)
paper doilies, gummed stickers and seals
seed catalogues, magazines, calendars (for cutting out pictures)
paper drinking straws

WHERE TO GET PAPERCRAFT SUPPLIES

It's going to be cheap and easy. For one thing, you already have some of the materials around the house: scissors, ruler, paper clips, clothespins, typing paper, and possibly a good many more items.

For another thing, one of the best sources of supply is your neighborhood 5-and-10. Shopping in the 5-and-10 keeps the amount of time and money you spend to a minimum. You will find there all the common kinds of paper—tissue, construction paper, gift-wrap, notepapers, typing paper, crepe paper, and Kraft paper. Some 5-and-10s even have small art supply departments where you can locate posterboard, bond and newsprint pads, paints, and brushes. Check out the hardware department for a mat knife and blades, the stationery department for glue, the housewares department for shelf paper and doilies.

What you can't find at the 5-and-10, you can find at any good art supply store. That's the place to pick up the more unusual kinds of paper—like rice paper, tableau paper, origami paper, metallic paper, and Aurora paper—as well as the heavier Bristol board, Bainbridge board, and chipboard. Art supply stores carry metal rulers, X-acto knives and blades, mat knives, single-edge razor blades, and bulldog clips, not to mention all kinds of paints and brushes.

If you still haven't collected everything you need, there are 4 more possibilities. Your next stop should be a hobby and craft supply store. Tell them what papers, knives, cords, and sequins you need and, while you're waiting for the salesperson to produce them, poke around for pretty decorative materials like decoupage prints and gold foil lace. When the hobby shop has been exhausted, proceed to a large stationery store. Look for a wide selection of giftwraps, tissue paper, and, of course, glue scissors, and the like. The third possibility is the hardware store, which will surely have a mat knife or utility knife, single-edge blades, and a carpenter's square or triangle.

I hate to think that after all this patient searching you might still be swimming aimlessly—but if you are, here comes the lifeboat: the mail-order house. Send for a catalogue and browse at leisure.

Sax Arts and Crafts Catalogue

P.O. Box 2002, Milwaukee, Wisconsin, 53201. Phone: (414)272-4900. Catalogue costs $1.00; minimum order is $7.50.

Papers: construction; Kraft; tissue; metallic; crepe; flint; origami; tracing; parchment; bond; oatmeal; newsprint; charcoal; pastel; tableau; rice (minimum quantities).

Dr. Martin's concentrated watercolors; brushes; bulldog clips; single-edge razor blades; knives and blades; glue; scissors; compass; triangle; paper punch; rulers; cords; sequins; spangles.

Dick Blick Creative Materials for Artist and Teacher

P.O. Box 1267, Galesburg, Illinois, 61401. Phone: (309)343-6181. Catalogue is free; no minimum order.

Papers: selection includes almost every paper mentioned in this book, but some papers and boards are available only in minimum quantities. Check it out; you might want to split an order with a friend.

Scissors; knives and blades; glue; brushes; rulers; triangles; compasses.

Vanguard Crafts

2915 Avenue J, Brooklyn, New York, 11210. Phone: (212)377-5188. Catalogue costs $.50; minimum order is $10.00 ($2.00 handling charge for orders between $5.00 and $10.00).

Papers: construction; tissue; crepe; newsprint; Kraft; origami; flint; oaktag (large quantities); railroad board.

Spools of wire; gold foil decorations; knives and blades; wire cutters; pipe cleaners; paper punch; brushes; sequins; spangles.

Boin Arts and Crafts Company

87 Morris Street, Morristown, New Jersey, 07960. Phone: (201)539-0600. Catalogue costs $1.00; minimum order is $5.00.

Papers: gold paper lace; tissue; pastel; rice; metallic foil; construction; newsprint; tracing; crepe; origami; Bainbridge #172; railroad board; oaktag.

Wire; pipe cleaners; cords; brushes; glue; oil paints; acrylic paints; X-acto knives and blades; bulldog clips; compass; straight edges; rulers; triangles.

Craft Service

337 University Avenue, Rochester, New York, 14607. Phone: (716)325-5547. Catalogue costs $.50; no minimum order.

Papers: construction; charcoal; bond; Bristol; tracing; newsprint; tableau; crepe; tissue; origami.

Cords; glue; beads; light wire; spangles; wire cutters; brushes; scissors; X-acto knives and blades.

Lewiscraft Mail Order Arts, Crafts, and Needlework Catalogue

40 Commander Boulevard, Agincourt, Ontario, Canada, M1S 3S2. Phone: (416) 291-8406. Catalogue costs $1.00; minimum order is $5.00.

Papers: construction; newsprint; tissue; crepe; Kraft; tracing; pastel; watercolor; rice; Bristol; metallic foil; boards; doilies; cards and envelopes.

Cords; wire; wire cutters; knives and blades; scissors; rulers; compass; carpenter's square; glue; tape; brushes; acrylic and oil paints; beads; sequins; spangles; feathers; pipe cleaners; straws.

SHOPPER'S GUIDE

The Shopper's Guide lists every material mentioned in the book. Use it for quick reference when you know exactly what you need and you want to find out where to get it.

ACRYLIC PAINT—art supply store
AURORA PAPER—art supply store

BAINBRIDGE BOARD—art supply store
BALLOONS—5-and-10
BEADS—5-and-10, hobby and craft store
BOND PAPER (pads)—art supply store
BOND PAPER (typing paper)—5-and-10, stationery store
BRISTOL BOARD—art supply store
BRUSHES (for applying glue)—5-and-10, hardware store, hobby and craft store
BULLDOG CLIPS (letter clips)—5-and-10, stationery store, art supply store

CHARCOAL PAPER—art supply store
CHIPBOARD—art supply store, hobby and craft store
CLOTHESPINS—5-and-10
COLORAID PAPER—art supply store
COLORED PENCILS—art supply store, 5-and-10, hobby and craft store
COMPASS—5-and-10, stationery store, art supply store
CONSTRUCTION PAPER—5-and-10, art supply store, hobby and craft store
COTTON STRING—5-and-10, stationery store, hardware store
CREPE PAPER (folded rolls and streamers)—5-and-10, party shop, hobby and craft store
CROCHET COTTON—5-and-10, needlework store

DECOUPAGE PRINTS—hobby and craft store
DOILIES—5-and-10, housewares store
DOWELS—hardware store, lumber yard, hobby and craft store

ELMER'S GLUE-ALL—5-and-10, hardware store, art supply store, hobby and craft store, stationery store
ENVELOPES—5-and-10, stationery store, card shop

FEATHERS—hobby and craft store, 5-and-10
FELT-TIP MARKERS—hobby and craft store, 5-and-10, art supply store

FLINT PAPER—art supply store
FOLDED NOTES—5-and-10, card shop
FRAME (do-it-yourself type)—5-and-10, hobby and craft store

GAFFER TAPE—hardware store, 5-and-10
GIFTWRAP—5-and-10, card shop, stationery store
GIFTWRAP (imported)—import store, art supply store
GLUE—5-and-10, hardware store, art supply store, hobby and craft store, stationery store
GUM ERASER (Artgum eraser)—5-and-10, art supply store, stationery store
GUMMED STICKERS—5-and-10, stationery store, hobby and craft store

HEAVY-DUTY THREAD—5-and-10

JAPANESE PRINTED PAPER—import store, art supply store

KNIT-CRO-SHEEN—5-and-10, needlework store
KRAFT PAPER—5-and-10, art supply store, stationery store

LACE—5-and-10, sewing supply store

MACRAME CORD—hobby and craft store, needlework store
MASKING TAPE—5-and-10, hardware store, stationery store
MAT BOARD—art supply store, framing shop
MAT KNIFE AND BLADES—art supply store, hardware store, hobby and craft store
METAL STRAIGHT EDGE (ruler, carpenter's square or triangle)—art supply store, hardware store
METALLIC FOIL PAPER—hobby and craft store, art supply store
METALLIC PAPER—art supply store
METALLIC PAPER LACE—hobby and craft store

NEEDLES—5-and-10
NEWSPRINT PAPER—art supply store, 5-and-10
NOTE PAPER—5-and-10, card shop

Papercraft Supplies

OAKTAG—5-and-10, art supply store, hobby and craft store, stationery store
OATMEAL PAPER—art supply store
OIL PAINT—art supply store, hobby and craft store
ORIGAMI PAPER—art supply store, hobby and craft store, import store

PAINT BRUSHES—hobby and craft store, art supply store, 5-and-10
PANTONE PAPER—art supply store
PAPER CLIPS—5-and-10, stationery store
PAPER PUNCH—5-and-10, stationery store
PARCHMENT PAPER—art supply store
PASTEL PAPER—art supply store
PEARL COTTON—5-and-10, needlework store
PINKING SHEARS—5-and-10, sewing supply store
PIPE CLEANERS—5-and-10, hobby and craft store, tobacconist
POSTER BOARD—art supply store, 5-and-10, hobby and craft store

RAILROAD BOARD—art supply store, hobby and craft store, 5-and-10
RHINESTONES—5-and-10, hobby and craft store, needlework store
RIBBON (cloth)—5-and-10, sewing supply store
RIBBON (ribbed giftwrapping type)—5-and-10, card shop
RICE PAPER—art supply store, import store
RICKRACK—5-and-10, sewing supply store
ROASTING PAN (aluminum)—5-and-10, housewares store
RULER (metal)—art supply store
RULER (plastic, wood)—5-and-10, stationery store

SCISSORS—5-and-10, stationery store, housewares store
SCOTCH TAPE—5-and-10, stationery store
SEQUINS—5-and-10, hobby and craft store, sewing supply store
SHELF PAPER—5-and-10, housewares store
SINGLE-EDGE RAZOR BLADES—art supply store, hardware store

SPANGLES—5-and-10, hobby and craft store, sewing supply store
SPEED-CRO-SHEEN—5-and-10, needlework store
STAMP PAD—stationery store, 5-and-10
STATIONERY—5-and-10, card shop
STRAWS (paper, for drinking)—5-and-10, housewares store
STREAMERS (ready-made, plain paper type)—5-and-10, party shop
STRING—5-and-10, stationery store, hardware store

TABLEAU PAPER—art supply store, hobby and craft store
TAG BOARD—art supply store, 5-and-10, hobby and craft store
TAPE MEASURE—5-and-10, sewing supply store
TISSUE PAPER—5-and-10, card shop, art supply store, hobby and craft store
TRACING PAPER—art supply store, stationery store
TRIANGLES (all types)—art supply store
T-SQUARE—art supply store
TURPENTINE—hardware store, paint store, 5-and-10, art supply store
TYPING PAPER—5-and-10, stationery store

UTILITY KNIFE—hardware store, 5-and-10

VASELINE—drugstore, 5-and-10

WATERCOLOR PAINT (concentrated, Dr. Martin's or Luma brands)—art supply store
WATERCOLOR PAINTBOXES—5-and-10, art supply store
WATERCOLOR PAPER—art supply store
WIRE (spooled)—5-and-10, hobby and craft store
WIRE CUTTERS—hardware store, 5-and-10

X-ACTO KNIFE AND BLADES—art supply store, hobby and craft store

YARN—5-and-10, needlework store

2. PLAIN & FANCY: MAKING PATTERNED PAPER

When you make a paper ornament from paper you have patterned yourself, it's like making potpourri from roses you have grown yourself. Double pleasure. Double pride. In fact, it's what the experts call craft satisfaction.

Any solid color paper can be patterned, but some papers work especially well with certain techniques. You will find these papers specified in the **Materials** listings.

Before you begin any decorating technique be sure that the paper you have chosen is flat and uncurled. If the paper is creased or very curled, iron it flat with a dry iron: Set the iron at the lowest heat, spread the paper on an ironing board, and iron gently. If creases don't come out, turn the heat a little higher and iron again. Increase the heat until the paper irons flat. Be careful of scorching. Remember, any paper that has been folded for a long time—like giftwrap—will retain some crease marks no matter how long you iron it. There's nothing you can do about those marks except ignore them.

SPATTER DECORATING

Materials: Any white or light-colored paper except those with glossy surfaces; toothbrush; several colors of concentrated watercolor paints (Luma or Dr. Martin's brand); paper cups, small glasses, or dishes; paper doilies, leaves, or construction paper (optional).

1. Put a dropperful of concentrated watercolor into a cup and dilute with 1 or 2 tablespoons of water, depending on how pale or brilliant you want the spattering to be. Mix well.

2. Dip the bristles of the toothbrush into the diluted color; tap the toothbrush to shake off excess drops. Spatter the paper: Hold the toothbrush about 1 ½" above the paper, with bristles pointing down, and flick your fingertip over the bristles. A fine spray of color will fall on the paper.

Suggestions

1. Spatter the paper with several colors, cleaning the toothbrush with soap and water between color changes.
2. Try spattering over interesting shapes or cut-outs: doilies, leaves, paper snowflakes, or geometric shapes cut from construction paper. Iron the cut-outs first if they are creased, then simply lay them down on the paper in a random design. Weight them with pennies or pebbles and spatter generously. When the spattering is dry, remove the shapes.

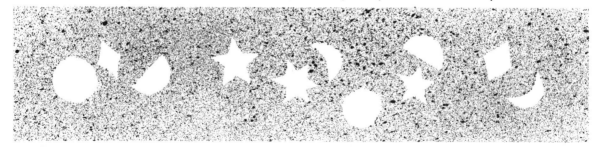

3. If you are spattering with 1 color, try starting with very diluted color and adding a few more drops of color to the cup each time you dip the toothbrush. This will give you a constantly deepening color—for example, from pink to red, lavender to violet, pale green to dark green.
4. If you are using an absorbent paper like tableau or newsprint, you can get a soft, mottled effect by spraying the paper with water from a plant-mister or laundry-sprayer before spattering.

DIP-IN-DYE DECORATING

Materials: Tableau paper (buy several sheets because dip-in-dye is so much fun that once you start you won't want to stop); several colors of concentrated watercolor paints (Luma or Dr. Martin's); small bowls or a muffin tin; newspapers spread out for drying the finished papers.

1. Make several colors—take them straight from the bottles or mix to get new ones: For each color put 5 or more drops of concentrated watercolor into either a small bowl or 1 compartment of the muffin tin; add 1 tablespoon of water to dilute the color and mix well. NOTE: The colors will dry lighter than they appear to be when wet, so keep them strong or be prepared for a pastel color range.

2. Cut 1 sheet of tableau paper into quarters, keeping the other sheets full size or cut in halves. I like to experiment with the quarter-sheets before going on to dyeing the larger sheets.
    Fold a quarter-sheet in half lengthwise and accordion-fold it into a long, narrow strip. Try to make the folds come out even. Fold the long strip in half and accordion-fold it into squares or triangles.

3. Dip each corner into a different color, allowing the dye to seep into the paper for a few seconds. Carefully unfold the paper and lay it on the newspapers to dry. When the paper is dry, iron it flat.

Suggestions

1. Dip only 1 or 2 corners in the dye.
2. To increase the absorbency, dip any corner in plain water before dipping it in dye.
3. Dip a corner in a light color for several seconds. When the color stops spreading, re-dip only the tip in a dark color.
4. Dip 1 corner in plain water only and the opposite corner in dye.
5. Dip the whole <u>edge</u> of 1 side into dye. Then you might go ahead and dip the corners too.
6. Hold a corner firmly with your thumb and forefinger when you dip it in the dye. The color will edge up around your fingers and remain very light where your fingers are. Then, without holding the corner, you might re-dip only the tip in a darker color.

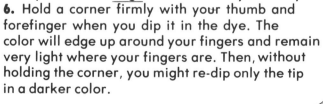

PAINTED PLEAT DECORATION

To make linear patterns, paper is folded in narrow pleats, painted along the folds, repleated, and painted again.

Materials: Absorbent paper like newsprint or tableau; several colors of concentrated watercolor paint (Luma or Dr. Martin's brand); muffin tin or paper cups for mixing paint; large paintbrush; jars of clean water for rinsing the brush; newspaper spread out for drying the finished designs.

1. Make 6 or 8 different colors. For each color, put 2 droppers of concentrated watercolor into either a paper cup or 1 compartment of a muffin tin. Dilute with a teaspoon of water and mix well.

2. Pleat a sheet of absorbent paper in 1 of the ways shown. Clip together all the folds of 1 side, using bulldog clips or clothespins. NOTE: Diagonal or fan-shaped pleats produce dynamic patterns; horizontal and vertical folds make stripes and plaids.

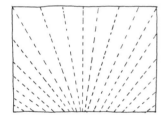 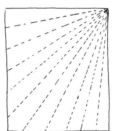 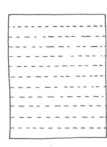 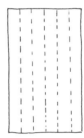 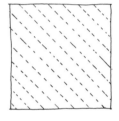

3. Brush paint along the unclipped folds in a sweeping motion; don't be timid about it. It's perfectly all right if some of the paint runs down between the pleats.

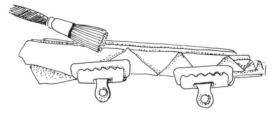

4. Remove the clips, unfold the paper and very gently—to avoid tearing—refold the paper in another direction. Repeat the painting process. Stop now or continue pleating and painting until you have a design you like.

5. When you are finished, unfold the paper carefully and spread it out on newspapers. Iron it when it is dry.

Suggestions

1. Brushing plain water on the folds before painting with color gives plumper, spreading lines.
2. Combine painted pleat decoration with spatter decoration.

STAMPED DECORATION

To make repeating patterns, cut a simple design in a gum eraser, ink it on a stamp pad, and print it on paper.

Materials: Any solid color paper; 1 or more gum or "Artgum" erasers; an ordinary stamp pad (more than 1 if you would like to print with more than 1 color); scrap paper.

1. With a ballpoint pen, draw a simple design on the end of the gum eraser. When you plan a design, keep in mind that the uncut parts of the eraser will be the parts inked on the stamp pad and printed on paper. Use an X-acto knife to cut away the areas outside the design and the extraneous parts within the design.

  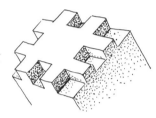

2. Press the stamper into the stamp pad and practice printing it on scrap paper. You will see that the stamper need not be heavily inked in order to make crisp, clear prints. When you finish the practice session, print a random or planned pattern all over the solid color paper.

Suggestions

1. A simple geometric shape can be extremely flexible.

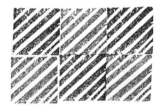

2. Make a patchwork pattern: Cut 4 different designs and alternate them.

3. A combination of stampers can make up 1 design.

MARBLEIZED PAPER

The basic procedure is to float several colors of oil paint on water in a pan and then gently lift the colors from the water's surface with a piece of paper.

Materials: Any solid color paper; several tubes (different colors) of oil paint; turpentine; brushes; jars or plastic containers for mixing paint (use containers you won't need again); large, disposable aluminum roasting pan; rags; newspapers.

1. Marbleizing is a messy technique so spread newspapers on the work surface and floor. Set the roasting pan in the middle of the work surface and fill the pan with a couple of inches of water. Keep rags handy for emergencies.

2. Cut a dozen pieces of paper, each the size of the bottom of the roasting pan or smaller. Marbleize these pieces until you have become fairly expert. Then work with larger pieces of paper, marbleizing them in sections.

3. Prepare several colors of paint, using a different container for each color. Each color is made with a ½ " squeeze of paint and ¼ cup of turpentine mixed together with a brush. The mixture should be a watery consistency. The amount of paint and turpentine needed to produce this consistency may vary according to the brand of paint and the intensity of color that you want; add more paint or turpentine as needed.

4. Float 3 colors of paint on the surface of the water like this: Dip a brush in a paint container, loading it with color. Splatter drops of paint onto the water by holding the brush over the edge of the roasting pan and tapping the brush against the edge. (If the paint sinks to the bottom of the pan, add more turpentine to the paint; the drops should hit the surface and stay there.)

As you splatter the different colors you will find that they behave differently; some spread, some sit in little drops, some in big drops. When all 3 colors are splattered, marble them slightly by drawing the top of the brush handle through the water very gently 2 or 3 times. NOTE: In the water, the colors appear to be weak and the marbling insignificant; when you apply the paper, you will find that the colors are strong and well-marbled.

5. Immediately after marbling the paint, take 1 of the prepared pieces of paper and hold it at each end, hovering over the water. Gently lay the paper down on the surface of the water and quickly lift it up again. The paper should stay on the surface only long enough to pick up the marbled paint, not long enough to become water-saturated.

Continue to hold the paper horizontal, parallel to the surface of the water. Do not tilt it; allow the excess water to drip off in this position. Then flip the paper over, paint side up, and set it on the newspapers to dry overnight.

Repeat this process as many times as you like, experimenting with different colors and ways of marbling. There is no need to change the water. When you are completely finished working, be sure to clean the brushes thoroughly with turpentine and then with soap and cold water.

LEAF PRINT DECORATION

Materials: Any solid color paper; small, fresh leaves; an ordinary stamp pad (more than 1 if you would like to print in more than 1 color); plastic wrap; tweezers; scrap paper.

1. Place a leaf on the stamp pad and cover it with a piece of plastic wrap. Gently rub the leaf through the plastic to ink up the leaf.

2. Lift the plastic and remove the leaf with tweezers. Place the leaf, ink side down, on the paper and cover it with a piece of scrap paper. Gently rub the leaf through the paper to print the leaf. Repeat this printing process all over the paper. Print randomly or in an orderly pattern.

3. PAPER-CUTTING

When the winter holidays roll around, the windows of elementary schools begin to frost over with decorations made of cut paper. When I was a school-child, my favorite decoration was the snowflake—a square of white paper folded into sixths, snipped, trimmed, and finally unfolded to display the magical transformation.

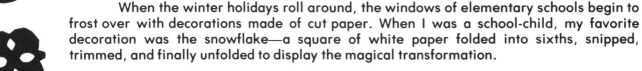

This chapter is about fold-and-cut techniques: single-fold cutting, double- and triple-fold cutting, and accordion folds.

Fold-and-cut techniques demand a thin paper that creases sharply and is easy to cut through several layers. For snowflakes and single-fold cuts, construction paper and typing paper are fine. You might also like thin charcoal and pastel papers, Aurora paper and other papers that are "colored 1 side only." More complicated paper-cuts need a thinner paper like origami paper, which I prefer for almost all double- and triple-fold cutting. Flint paper and giftwrap work well, too.

For cutting, you must use the small pointy scissors mentioned in Chapter 1; large scissors won't do. The X-acto knife will come in handy, and, of course, you have a ruler, glue, and a small brush for the glue.

You will find within this chapter many ideas for things to cut: apples, birds, butterflies, flowers, geometric patterns. Undoubtedly, you will have ideas of your own, but if you do run out of steam, there are many sources of ideas available to you. For example, gardening catalogues have pictures of exotic flowers, vegetables, and fruits. Photos and illustrations in magazines, calendars, and children's books will suggest other design possibilities. The library has books on folk art, border designs, costumes, needlework, birds, insects, and plants, any one of which may inspire you.

Finished paper-cuts are delicate, often intricate, and can't be hung up or handed round in their natural states. They need to be mounted or framed. Suggestions and complete instructions for mounting and framing are at the end of this chapter.

SINGLE-FOLD CUTTING

I like 2 kinds of single-fold paper-cutting. One is the simple cutting of figures, animals, Easter eggs, etc., which may then have some cutting within them. The other kind is Polish paper-cutting, which you see in flower form on the book jacket.

Simple Cutting

Take a square of paper, fold it in half, and draw half of a design or figure. Cut out the design and unfold the paper.

NOTE: Sketchy pencil lines can be confusing when you proceed to cut out the design. Clarify the design before cutting by lightly shading (with pencil) the sections to be cut out.

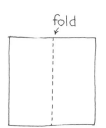 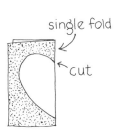 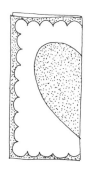 

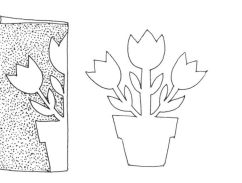 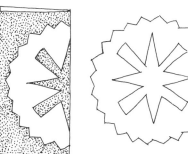  

27

Take it a step further: Fold a square of paper in half and draw half of a design; draw some shapes <u>within</u> the design. Cut out the shapes within the design first, then cut out the design itself. When planning cut-outs within a design, remember that the fold holds everything together; if you detach any part completely from every other part, it will fall out.

Some designs are better suited to being cut from folded diamonds, rectangles, or circles.

Backing with contrasting papers

If you think your single-fold figures and designs are not fancy enough to deserve framing, dress them up with color: Back the openings in the paper-cut with pieces of contrasting paper, giftwrap, patterned paper, or metallic paper. Here's how to do it.

Place the paper-cut right side up on a contrasting paper. With pencil, draw around an opening. Remove the paper-cut. Cut out the drawing 1/8" from the pencil line. If there are many openings in the paper-cut, you can simply draw around all of them on a single piece of contrasting paper and cut 1/8" outside the outermost pencil line.

Turn the paper-cut wrong side up. With a small brush, carefully apply slightly diluted glue to either the edges of an opening or the edges of a backing piece. Then press the paper-cut in place on top of the backing piece, or press the backing piece in place on the back of the paper-cut. Smooth out carefully. Repeat this process until all the backing pieces are glued in position.

draw around the opening

contrasting paper

cut out 1/8" outside pencil line

wrong side

brush glue on

wrong side

press paper-cut in place

right side

Polish Paper-Cutting

This folk art is a fooler. The intricate flowers, leaves,
and borders appear to have been cut with magic scissors.
In fact, the Polish people have traditionally used sheep shears.

Each flower is composed of several individually-cut layers; the leaves and borders
are cut separately. When all the elements are ready, the design is glued together piece by
piece on another sheet of paper. A simple design can be 1 flower on a stem with 2 leaves.
A more complicated design might be 3 to 5 flowers on a stem with 4 to 6 leaves flanked by
roosters with feathery tails and the whole arrangement sitting on a lacy border.

Use origami paper for Polish paper-cutting because it is thin enough to be cut with
great precision and because it comes in a rich variety of colors. If you want a really authen-
tic look, be sure to incorporate many colors and also the characteristic notching and shapes
of traditional Polish paper-cutting.

1. Fold a 4 ½" square of green paper in half. Draw half of the main stem, 2 smaller stems, and 2 leaves. The leaves in the drawing are the characteristic notched shapes of Polish paper-cut leaves. Cut on the pencil line and unfold the paper.

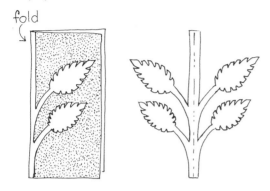

NOTE: To cut out a shape with a notched edge, first cut out the entire shape without notches. Then cut the notches in the smooth edge.

2. Fold a 2 ½" square of brightly colored paper in half. Draw 1 half of the head of a flower. Cut on the pencil line and unfold the paper.

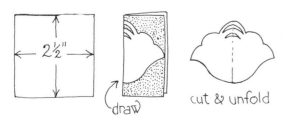

3. Make the first layer for the flower: Choose a piece of paper of another color and fold it in half. Outline 1 half of the head of the flower, lining up the center fold line of the flower with the fold line of the new piece of paper. Remove the flower and draw half of a flower shape (no stem) within the outline. Cut on the pencil line and unfold the paper.

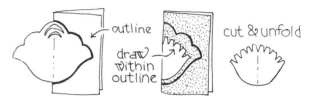

4. Cut 2 or 3 more layers, using different colors of paper. Always draw the outline of the previous layer as a guide, keeping within the outline when drawing and cutting a new layer.

5. Cut 1 layer for the leaves, using lighter or darker green paper: Fold the paper in half and outline the leaves on it. Draw a smaller leaf within each outline. Cut out the new leaves; you should have 4 altogether.

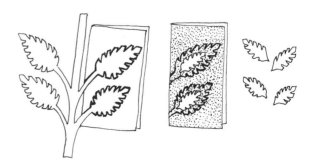

6. When all the layers and leaves are cut, glue the parts together, using slightly diluted glue and a small brush. Start with the head of the flower: Glue 1 layer on the other in the order in which you cut them, lining up the center fold lines; carefully smooth down each layer and wipe off excess glue.

Next choose a square of contrasting paper to mount the stem, leaves, and flower on; be sure the square is large enough to accomodate the height of the flower and the width of the leaves. With pencil, mark the center line of the square.

Apply glue to the back of the main stem and position it on the square,

lining up the center fold with the pencil line. Glue down the other stems and the leaves. Now apply glue to the back of the flower head and press it in position on the main stem. Finally, glue the layers on the leaves.

ACCORDION-FOLD CUTTING

Accordion-fold cutting produces chains of identical birds, flowers, geometric shapes, people. Long chains can be used as Christmas tree decorations and as borders and decorations on boxes, cards, notes, and books. Short chains can be backed with colored papers (see page 29) and then mounted and framed.

Cut a strip of paper and fold it into 4 or 8 parts. Always fold along the grain when you are using paper with a definite grain. For example, construction paper, bond paper, and Aurora paper have pronounced grains; tissue paper and origami paper do not. Find the grain by folding the paper first in 1 direction and then the opposite; the paper folds easily along the grain and resists folding across the grain.

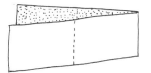

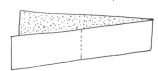

fold in half & then in 4 parts OR fold in half, then in 4 parts, then in 8 parts

Draw the design on the top part, making sure that the design extends all the way to the folds OR that the design is halved by the folds. (NOTE: Use pencil to shade the sections to be cut out before you actually cut them.) Cut out the design and unfold the chain.

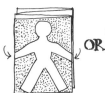

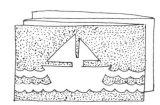

OR

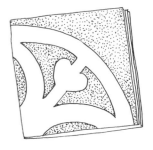

DOUBLE-FOLD CUTTING

Double-fold cutting is perfect for making square designs and circular designs.

Fold a square of paper in half and then in quarters. Draw a design, pencilling in the areas to be cut out. Cut out the design (pencilled areas <u>within</u> the larger areas should be cut first) and unfold carefully.

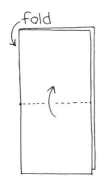

fold

fold

draw

cut

cut

Mount or frame the design after reading the information on pages 38 through 40.

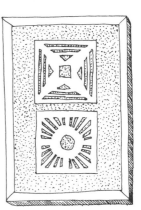

TRIPLE-FOLD CUTTING

Use this fold-and-cut technique to produce delicate, intricate doilies.

Fold a square in half, then in quarters, and finally in eighths. Cut off the outer points, making them rounded for a circle or shaped for 8 "petals."

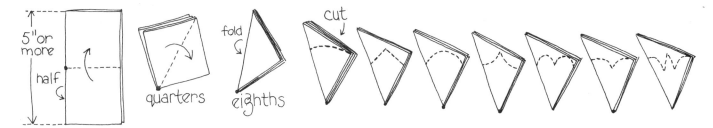

Draw the design and pencil in the areas to be cut out. Cut them out carefully—these areas are apt to be tiny and hard to get at. Give the doily a final, finished look by cutting the outer edge into a notched, scalloped, or other pattern.

Mount or frame the doily after reading the information on pages 38 through 40.

MOUNTING AND FRAMING THE FINISHED PAPER-CUT

The best way to show off a finished paper-cut is to mount or frame it and hang it on the wall. Mounting means gluing the paper-cut onto a piece of paper that will display the paper-cut to advantage. If you want to frame it, do so <u>after</u> you have mounted it in one of the ways suggested below.

◆ Mount on a sheet of paper slightly larger than the paper-cut.

◆ Mount on a series of pieces of paper, each slightly larger than the one before. This creates a border of narrow stripes around the paper-cut.

◆ Mount the paper-cut first on a piece of paper that is exactly the same size as the paper-cut: Outline the paper-cut on the mounting paper and cut out on the pencil line; then mount on a slightly larger piece.

◆ Back some of the openings of the paper-cut with papers of contrasting colors (see page 29) and then mount on a larger sheet.

◆ Mount several paper-cuts on the same sheet of paper. Mark the placement carefully with pencil before mounting.

How to Mount a Paper-Cut

The first step is choosing a paper for the mounting. If you are planning to stiffen the mounted paper-cut later by framing it or gluing it to board (as described in the next section, "The Follow-Up"), then any of these papers would be good choices for the mounting: origami paper; charcoal and pastel papers; construction paper; Aurora paper or other papers "colored 1 side only"; flint paper; bond paper. If you are <u>not</u> planning to frame the mounted paper-cut or glue it to board, then mount on posterboard or 4-ply Bristol board.

When you decide on the type of mounting paper, pick a contrasting—but not <u>too</u> contrasting—color; watch out for contrasting colors that vibrate next to the color of the paper-cut. For example, mounting a bright red paper-cut on a piece of bright green paper will result in a jumping, flashing optical effect that makes it hard to see the paper-cut. Experiment with different colors before making a final choice. Cut the mounting paper to the desired size.

Iron the paper-cut carefully between 2 pieces of scrap paper—use a dry iron on a low setting. Using a small brush, apply slightly diluted glue sparingly (but completely) to the wrong side of the center section of the paper-cut. Position the paper-cut correctly on the mounting paper and press down gently. Wipe off excess glue and allow to dry. Lift up another section of the paper-cut, carefully apply glue to the wrong side, and smooth down the section. Do this to each section. Allow the whole paper-cut to dry and then press in a heavy book. When the mounted paper-cut is flat, remove it from the book.

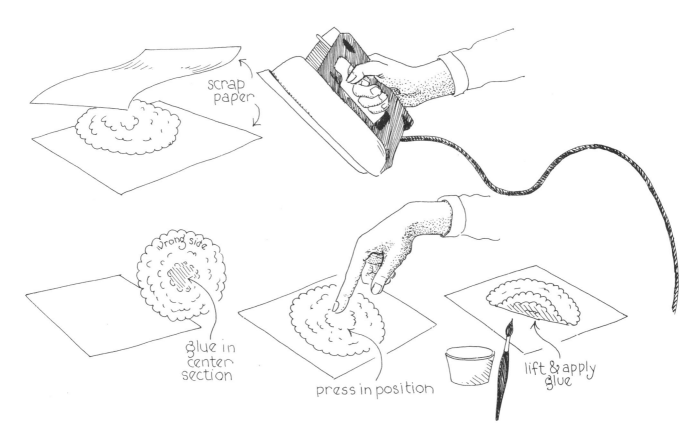

scrap paper

wrong side

glue in center section

press in position

lift & apply glue

The Follow-Up

After mounting, the paper-cut may then be glued to a board or framed in one of these ways.

◆ Glue a mounted paper-cut to a piece of plain cardboard. Since the cardboard is simply a stiffener for the paper-cut, do not leave a border around the paper-cut. Glue the mounted paper-cut to the cardboard and cut away the excess cardboard with a mat knife or single-edge razor blade. (Please read the instructions for cutting with mat knife or razor blade on page 83.)

◆ Glue a mounted paper-cut to white or colored mat board. Cut the mat board to the desired size, allowing a generous border around the paper-cut. With a pencil, mark the placement of the mounted paper-cut and glue it to the mat board.

◆ Frame the mounted paper-cut. Have it done professionally at a framing shop or stop at the 5-and-10 for an inexpensive wood frame (includes glass and cardboard backing) that you put together yourself.

 If you use a 5-and-10 frame, first glue the mounted paper-cut to a pretty piece of paper that fits the frame perfectly. Remove the cardboard backing from the frame, insert the mounted paper-cut and replace the cardboard. Hang the framed cut on the wall.

excess cardboard

4. FLOWERS

On my worktable, in a white enamel pitcher with blue trim, is a bouquet of summer flowers. They are pink, turquoise, yellow, and white — and they are made of paper.

These flowers are so easy to make that on a hot day I may take out some of the pink and yellow flowers and replace them with cool blues and lavenders. In the fall, I will make a new bunch — red, bright orange, peach, brown, and dark green for the leaves. I can have new flowers for every season and every occasion and so can you.

The materials you need for making flowers are tissue paper, crepe paper, pipe cleaners, light and heavy wire, wire cutters, and a small piece of tracing paper for 1 or 2 of the flowers.

The following information applies to all flower projects.

About paper

You will need a variety of colors of tissue and crepe paper. Remember, paper flowers do not have to be the colors of real flowers. However, they do seem to look best when you make the stems and leaves realistically green. I recommend that you include 1 or 2 shades of green when you are choosing paper.

About grain

If you take a piece of crepe paper and try to fold it first in 1 direction and then the other, you will see that it folds easily in 1 direction and resists folding in the other. This is because of the grain — any paper folds willingly along its grain. Tissue paper has negligible grain while crepe paper has a pronounced grain. Here is my rule with crepe paper: Always cut petals and leaves along the grain; that is, the length of the petal or leaf should run in the same direction as the grain. Strips that will be wound should be cut across the grain, that is, perpendicular to the grain.

About wire

When you buy heavy wire (and please note that heavy is a relative term — I'm not talking about wire hangers), choose spooled wire that will be strong enough when it is unwound and straightened out to stand up by itself and support a flower. Number 18 or 20 soft brass wire is a good choice.

When you buy light wire choose spooled or other wire about the weight of heavy thread. Beading wire works well.

About pinch-pleating

What is pinch-pleating? The whole story is right there in the words: pinch and pleat. To make tiny pleats — my dictionary defines pleats as flat folds, doubled over and held in place — just pinch up a little bit of paper and fold it over. Without letting go of the first pleat, pinch up a second pleat. Keep pinching and folding until you reach the end of the paper and your fingers are full of scrunched-up pleats.

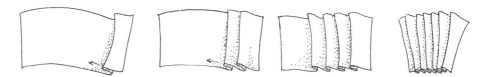

Showing off your finished flowers

Before you deposit your flowers in the nearest vase, consider these display possibilities.

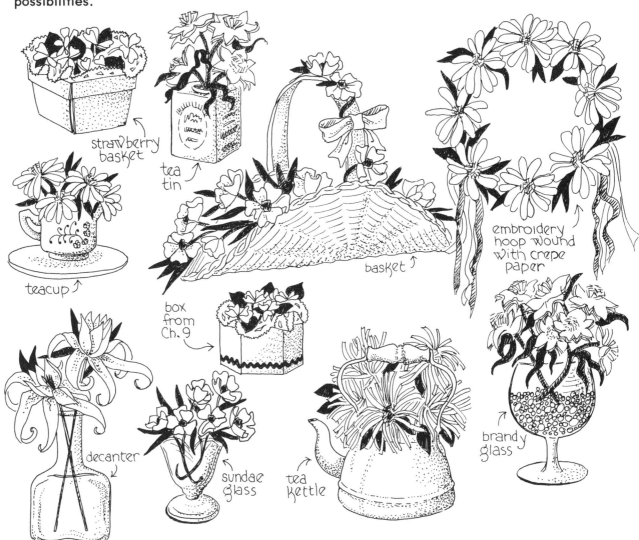

strawberry basket

tea tin

basket ↗

embroidery hoop wound with crepe paper

teacup ↗

box from Ch. 9 →

decanter

sundae glass

tea kettle

brandy glass

SIMPLE FLOWER AND VARIATION

Make flowers of all sizes using this general technique.
Measurements here are for 1 large flower.

Materials: Crepe paper (green plus 2 colors, Color A for the center of the flower and Color B for the petals); 8″ pipe cleaner or 8″ to 10″ piece of heavy wire; light wire.

Simple Flower

1. Prepare the center and stem: Cut a 4″ x 7″ strip of Color A crepe paper. (Note the direction of the grain.) Fold the strip and snip a fringe in both edges. Unfold and pinch-pleat tightly down the center. Secure the center with the end of a pipe cleaner (or piece of wire) as shown. NOTE: If you are making a small flower, use wire instead of pipe cleaner.

Push the fringes up and secure them by winding tightly with a piece of light wire. Twist the ends of the wire together.

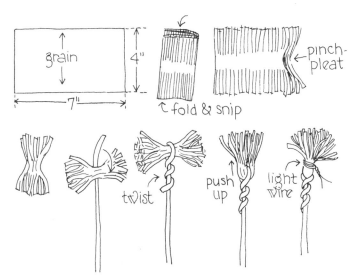

grain

4″

7″

fold & snip

pinch-pleat

twist

push up

light wire

2. Prepare the petals, leaves, and stem-winding strip.

Petals: Cut 2 strips of Color B crepe paper, each 4" x 12". Note the direction of the grain. Snip a fringe along 1 edge of each strip, leaving about 1" un-cut. The fringe may be wide or narrow, depending upon what kind of petals you prefer.

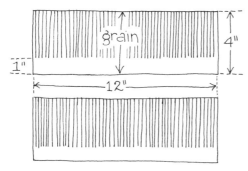

Leaves: Cut green crepe paper leaves in groups of 3. Choose 1 of the types shown below and cut 2 or 3 groups.

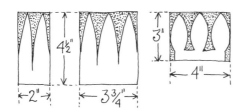

Stem-winding strip: Cut ½"-wide strip from the end of a folded roll of green crepe paper. You will be cutting across the grain through all the layers. Unfold the strip.

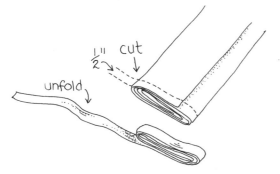

3. Glue the petals to the center and stem: Dab glue around the base of the center and down the stem a bit. Take the end of 1 strip of petals, position it on the base of the center, and begin to pinch-pleat the petals around the center. Dab more glue along the unfringed edge as you pleat — this keeps it secured firmly. When you have used up 1 strip of petals, repeat the process for the second strip. The petals will be sticking straight up; fluff them out later.

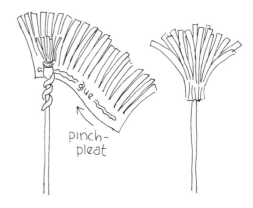

4. Cover the stem and add the leaves: Hold onto the petals firmly at the base. Dab glue around the base and begin winding the stem-strip tightly around the base. Wind around several times, adding more dabs of glue to secure the stem-strip.

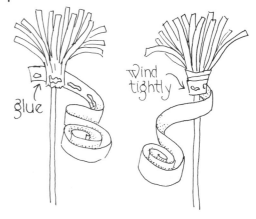

Spiral the stem-strip gradually down the stem, dabbing glue on the stem as you go. When you have wound for about ½" of the stem, add a group of leaves: Pinch-pleat the edge of a leaf group, hold it next to the stem with a dab of glue, and wind the stem-strip tightly around the pinched part. Wind down the stem for another ½", dabbing glue on the stem, and attach another leaf group in the same way. Continue spiralling the stem-strip tightly around the stem, dabbing glue and gradually working down the whole stem. Glue the strip at the bottom of the stem and cut off the excess. Fluff out the petals.

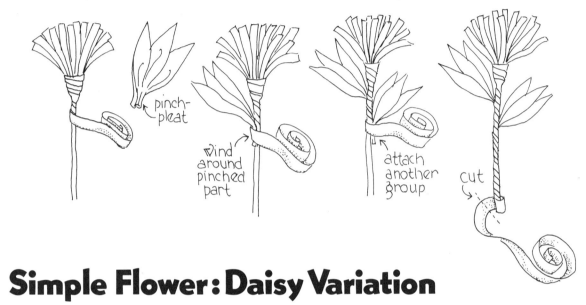

Simple Flower: Daisy Variation

Make the daisy in the same way as the Simple Flower, but substitute a different center, petals, and leaves.

Center: Cut a 2" x 5" strip of Color A crepe paper.

Petals: Cut 3 strips of Color B crepe paper, each 2 ½" x 6". Cut 10 petals in each strip, leaving about ½" uncut. The easiest way to do this is to stack the 3 strips, fold them in half, and cut 5 petals through all the layers.

Leaves: Cut 3 or 4 groups with 5 leaves in each group. Cut each group from a 2" x 3" piece of green crepe paper.

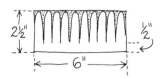

TROPICAL FLOWER

Materials: Crepe paper (green plus 2 colors, Color A for the center and Color B for the petals); 10" piece of heavy wire; light wire.

1. Prepare the center and stem: Cut a 2" x 2 ½" strip of Color A crepe paper and snip 1 edge into thin points. Dab glue along the end of the wire and along the bottom edge of the center. Roll the center tightly around the end of the wire.

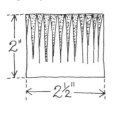
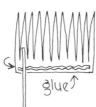

glue↑

2. Prepare the petals, leaves, and stem-winding strip.

   Petals: Cut 6 individual short petals and 6 individual long ones from Color B crepe paper. Each short petal is cut from a piece of crepe paper 1 ½" x 3 ½"; each long one is cut from a piece 1" x 5 ½". Be sure there is a tail on each petal, as shown. When all petals are cut, hold each petal flat and roll the tail between your thumb and forefinger to make the tail thin and twisted.

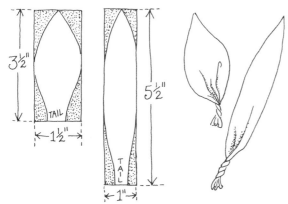

Leaves: Cut 2 or 3 groups of 3 leaves each. Cut each group from a 1 ½" x 4 ½" piece of green crepe paper.

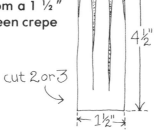

cut 2 or 3 →

Stem-winding strip: Cut a ½"-wide strip from the end of a folded roll of green crepe paper. You will be cutting across the grain through all layers. Unfold the strip.

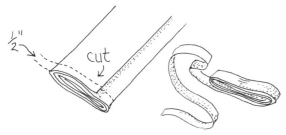

cut

3. Attach the petals to the center and stem: Group the short petals around the center and secure them in position with a piece of light wire wound tightly around the twisted tails. Group the long petals around the short ones and wire them in-place the same way. All the petals will be standing straight up; open and curl them later.

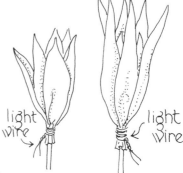

light wire   light wire

4. Cover the stem and add the leaves: Dab glue around the base of the petals and begin winding the stem-strip tightly around the base. Wind it around several times, adding dabs of glue to secure it well. Continue winding around the base until it is well covered.

Now add a leaf group: Pinch-pleat the edge of a leaf group, hold it next to the base with a bit of glue, and wind the stem-strip tightly around the pinched part. Spiral the stem-strip gradually down the stem for 2", dabbing on glue, and attach another leaf group. Continue winding, adding the last leaf group if you have one, dabbing glue on the stem. When you reach the end of the stem, glue the strip and cut off the excess.

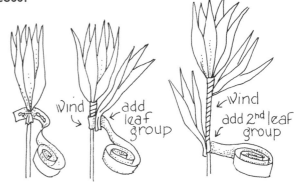

wind   add leaf group   wind   add 2nd leaf group

Fluff out all the petals and curl the long petals around a pencil.

CLUSTER OF CREPE PAPER FLOWERS

Materials: Crepe paper (green plus 1 other color); tissue paper (1 color); 1 pipe cleaner 8" long and 1 pipe cleaner cut in half; small piece of tracing paper.

1. Prepare the petals, leaves, and stem-winding strip.

Petals: To cut 15 petals, first trace the petal shown full size here. Stack 15 pieces of the other color of crepe paper; each piece should be a little larger than the full-sized petal shown. Lay the tracing on top of the stack and cut out the petal through all layers.

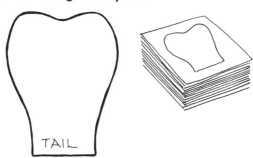

TAIL

Separate the petals. Hold each petal flat and roll the square tail of each petal between thumb and forefinger to make it thin and twisted.

Leaves: Cut 4 groups of 4 leaves each. Each group is cut from a piece of green crepe paper 1 ½ " x 3 ½ ".

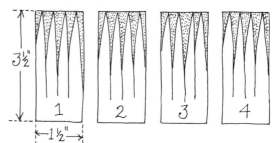

Stem-winding strip: Cut a ½"-wide strip from the end of a folded roll of green crepe paper. You will be cutting across the grain through all the layers. Unfold the strip.

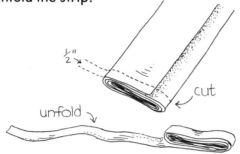

2. Each of the 3 pipe cleaners is 1 stem. Attach 5 petals to each stem as follows: Dab glue around the end of the stem. Group 5 petals around the stem with the twisted tails in the glue and the petals pointing up. Pinch the tails tightly to the stem. When the tails are secure, dab more glue around them and begin winding the stem-strip tightly around the tails. Continue spiralling the stem-strip gradually down the entire stem, dabbing more glue on the stem as you go. Glue the strip at the bottom of the stem and cut off the excess.

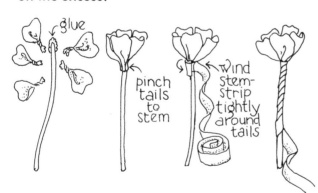

3. Make the centers of the flowers: Cut 3 pieces of tissue, each 1 ½" square, and scrunch each one into a ball. Open the petals of each flower, put a dab of glue in the center, and place a ball of tissue in the glue.

4. Attach the 3 flowers and the leaves together: Hold 1 short-stemmed flower next to the long-stemmed one, with some glue between them. Dab a bit more glue around the joint and wind the joint tightly with stem-strip. Pinch-pleat the edge of a group of leaves, hold it next to the stem with a dab of glue, and wind the stem-strip around the pinched part, catching the leaf group in the stem-winding process.

Continue spiralling the stem-strip gradually down the 2 joined stems for another ½", dabbing on more glue. Add another group of leaves. Wind the stem-strip for another ½" and attach the third flower in the same way you attached the second flower. Wind again for another ½" and add another group of leaves. Continue winding for 1 ½" and add the last group of leaves.

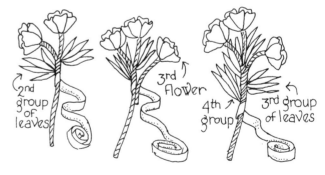

Finish spiralling the stem-strip gradually to the bottom of the stems, dabbing glue as you go. At the bottom, glue the strip and cut off the excess. Fluff out the petals.

NOSEGAY OF VIOLETS

Put together half a dozen tissue paper violets, a delicate tissue doily, and a crepe paper bow to make this small bouquet.

Materials: Tissue paper (green plus 2 colors, Color A for the petals and Color B for the doily); crepe paper (green plus 1 color for the bow); 3 or 4 8" pipe cleaners cut in half or 6 to 8 4" lengths of heavy wire; small piece of tracing paper.

Violets

The following instructions are for the petals and leaves of 1 violet. The stem-strip will be enough for all 6 or 8 violets in the nosegay.

1. Prepare petals, leaves, and stem-winding strip.

Petals: Trace the petal shown full size here and cut it out. Stack 4 small pieces of Color A tissue paper, lay the tracing on top of the stack, and cut out the petal through all the layers. (NOTE: Continue to use this same tracing paper pattern for all the violets that you make.) Hold each petal flat and carefully roll the tail of each petal to make it thin and twisted.

Leaves: Cut 2 leaves from green tissue, using the full-sized pattern as a guide. Roll the tails of the leaves as you did the tails of the petals.

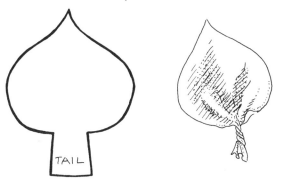

Stem-winding strip: Cut a ½"-wide strip from the end of a folded roll of green crepe paper. You will be cutting across the grain through all the layers. Unfold the strip.

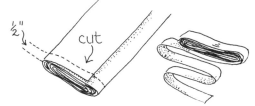

2. Attach the petals and leaves to the stem: First glue the petals together in pairs. Then dab glue on the end of a pipe cleaner or piece of heavy wire and press the pairs of petals into place as shown.

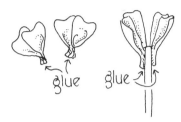

When the petals are secure, dab more glue around the tails and begin winding the stem-strip tightly around them. Wind gradually down ½" of the stem, dabbing on more glue. Now add a leaf: Hold the leaf next to the stem with a bit of glue and wind the stem-strip tightly around the tail of the leaf.

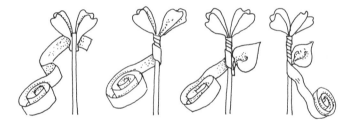

Continue winding down the stem, dabbing on more glue, for another ½" to 1". Attach the second leaf. Finish spiralling down the entire stem, dabbing more glue as you go. Glue at the bottom and cut off the excess stem-strip. Open out the petals and leaves.

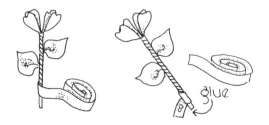

Make 5 to 7 more violets.

Doily

With pinking shears, cut a tissue paper circle about 7" in diameter. Fold it into eighths and use regular scissors to cut a simple design in the 2 folded edges. Do not cut below the 1 ½" mark except for snipping off the point of the wedge. Unfold the doily carefully.

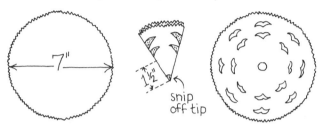

Putting the Nosegay Together

1. Slip the stems of the violets through the hole in the center of the doily. Pinch the doily tightly around the stems, dabbing some glue on the stems to hold the doily in position. Cut a 4" piece of stem-strip, dab some glue on the pinched doily and stems, and wrap the strip tightly around them.

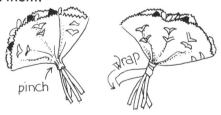

2. Cut a ½" x 18" strip of another color of crepe paper and make a bow as shown. Glue the bow to the wrapped stems. As a final touch, fluff out the doily and bend the violets in different directions.

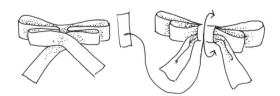

CLUSTER OF TISSUE PAPER FLOWERS

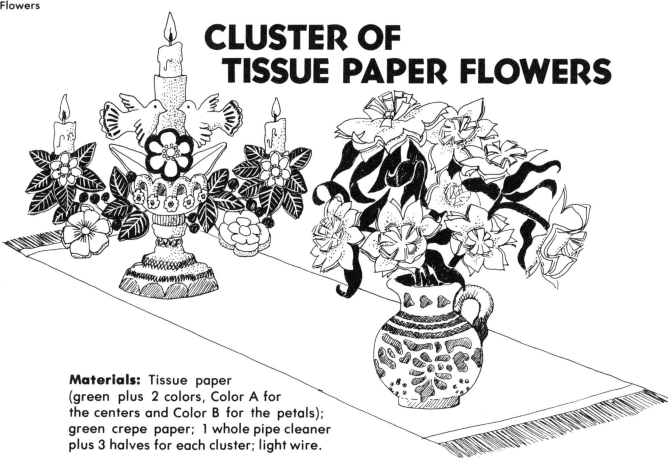

Materials: Tissue paper (green plus 2 colors, Color A for the centers and Color B for the petals); green crepe paper; 1 whole pipe cleaner plus 3 halves for each cluster; light wire.

1. A cluster is made up of 4 identical flower heads, 1 attached to a whole pipe cleaner and 3 attached to half pipe cleaners. Here are the instructions for making 1 flower head and for attaching it to a pipe cleaner stem.

Cut 3 pieces of Color B tissue paper, each 2 ½ " square. Stack them, fold them into quarters, and round off the corners. Cut the edge into petal shapes. Unfold.

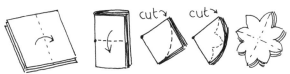

Cut 5 pieces of Color A tissue, each 1 ¼ " square. Fold and round off the corners. Unfold.

Stack the 2 groups of tissue together, centering the small circles on the larger ones. With a large needle make 2 holes, ¼ " apart, through all the layers of tissue. Put a piece of light wire through the holes, pull the ends even, and twist, pinching the layers of tissue upward to flute them slightly. Snip the edges of the smaller circles into fringe and fluff them out.

52

Place a pipe cleaner or half a pipe cleaner next to the base of the flower head and wind the light wire tightly to the pipe cleaner, attaching the flower head to the stem.

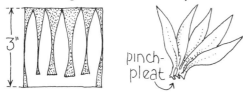

Repeat step 1 to make 3 more flowers.

2. Prepare the leaves and stem-winding strip.

Leaves: Make 4 groups of leaves (1 group for each flower) with 5 leaves in each group. Cut each group out of a 3" x 3" square of green tissue paper. Pinch-pleat the straight edge of each group and dab on some glue to secure the pleats.

3"

pinch-pleat

Stem-winding strip: Cut a ½"-wide strip from the end of a folded roll of green <u>crepe</u> paper. You will be cutting across the grain through all layers. Unfold the strip.

½" cut

3. Attach 1 group of leaves to each <u>short-stemmed</u> flower while you are winding the stem: Dab glue around the base of the flower and begin winding the stem-strip tightly around the base. Spiral gradually down the stem for about 1", dabbing on more glue. Hold the leaf group next to the stem, applying a bit of glue, and wind the stem-strip around the pinch-pleated part of the leaf group. Continue winding the stem-strip gradually down the entire stem, dabbing more glue as you go. Glue

the stem-strip at the bottom of the stem and cut off the excess. Repeat this process for the other 2 short-stemmed flowers.

4. Attach the short-stemmed flowers to the long-stemmed flower: Begin by dabbing glue around the base of the long flower and winding it tightly with stem-strip. Attach a leaf group as described in step 3. Wind for another ½" of stem, dabbing glue to secure the stem-strip.

Now take 1 of the short flowers and hold it next to the long flower with a bit of glue between the 2 stems. Dab more glue around the stems and wind the stem-strip tightly around the 2 stems. Continue spiralling gradually down 1" to 1 ½" of the stems and attach another flower in the same way. Wind down the stem for another 1 ½" and attach the last flower. Spiral gradually down the rest of the stem, glue at the bottom, and cut off the excess stem-strip.

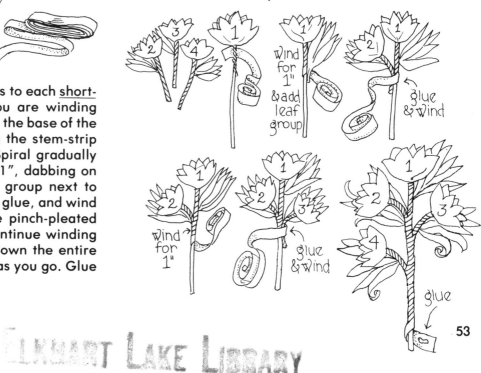

EXTRA BRANCHES OF LEAVES

If your bouquet of flowers looks a little skimpy, fill it out with some extra branches of leaves, just as a florist does. Branches may be made with groups of leaves or with individual leaves.

Materials: Green crepe paper; green tissue paper (optional); heavy wire or pipe cleaners; wire cutters.

Branches Made of Groups of Leaves

1. Prepare leaves and stem-winding strip.

Leaves: Cut groups of several leaves, using the drawings as guidelines. Cut several groups at a time by stacking pieces of crepe or tissue paper and cutting through all layers.

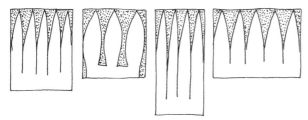

Stem-winding strip: Cut a ½"-wide strip from the end of a folded roll of green crepe paper. You will be cutting across the grain through all the layers. Unfold the strip.

2. Attach the leaves to the stem: Dab glue along the end of a pipe cleaner or length of heavy wire. Pinch-pleat the bottom edge of a group of leaves and press onto the gluey end of the pipe cleaner or wire. Dab a bit more glue around the pleated edge and begin winding the end of the stem-strip tightly around it. Continue winding down the stem for about ½" to 1", dabbing on more glue. Pinch-pleat another group of leaves, hold it next to the stem with a bit of glue, and wind the stem-strip tightly around the pinched part.

Continue winding and adding leaf groups at intervals. Do not attach any leaves below the half-way point. At that point, simply spiral the stem-strip to the bottom of the stem, glue the strip, and cut off the excess.

Branches Made of Individual Leaves

Make these in basically the same way you made branches with groups of leaves, but work with single leaves instead.

Using the drawings as guidelines, cut as many leaves as you like, always being sure that each leaf has a tail. When you have cut all the leaves, hold each leaf flat and roll the tail between your thumb and forefinger to make it thin and twisted.

Attach the leaves to pipe cleaners or wire stems, catching the twisted tails in the stem-winding process.

5. HANGING ORNAMENTS

I discovered the hanging ornament one day when the dozens of paper ornaments I was making turned into a small avalanche rushing over my entire worktable. In the limited space of my studio, the only place left to put the ornaments was in mid-air. So I tied a string from the top of the bookcase at one end of the room to a nail in the wall about 6 feet away and hung 20 of my favorite ornaments from the string. They looked so pretty that I left them there permanently. Discover for yourself the pleasures and possibilities of hanging paper ornaments.

◆ Hang paper ornaments on the Christmas tree and give a few ornaments to a friend for her tree.

◆ Hang some ornaments from the light fixture in the playroom or in the children's bedroom.

◆ Suspend an ornament from the bottom of a hanging plant.

◆ Cheer up a sick child with some ornaments hanging on a string tied from bedpost to bedpost.

◆ For Thanksgiving dinner or any other holiday feast, decorate the chandelier with hanging ornaments.

◆ Hang some from the birthday child's chair.

◆ Dangle ornaments from the Christmas mantelpiece along with the stockings.

◆ Make a mobile for a baby.

5 ways to hang an ornament

Attach a piece of thin string (like crochet cotton, yarn, or cotton wrapping string) to each ornament before tying it to the Christmas tree or anywhere else. Any of the 5 methods will work for almost any ornament.

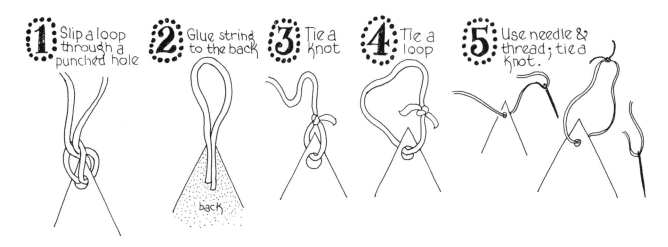

How to do scoring

The papercraft technique called scoring is used when you want to fold a heavy paper or thin board. Scoring means making a deep indentation or a shallow cut (just breaking but not cutting through the surface) along an indicated line. The paper or board then folds easily along the scored line. Use a blunt knife for making an indentation; use a mat knife, X-acto knife, or single-edge razor blade for making a shallow cut.

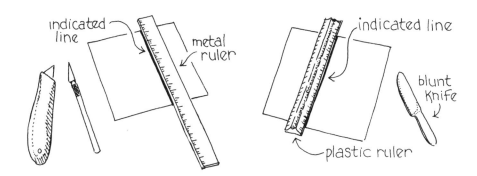

BIRD WITH PLEATED WINGS

Materials: Posterboard or 3- or 4-ply Bristol board; metallic foil paper or other thin paper.

Cut a bird out of posterboard, using the graph as a guide. Cut a slit as shown. For the wings, cut a 6" square of foil paper and pleat diagonally. Pinch the pleated square in the middle and fan out the ends. Slip the wings into the slit. Cut several narrow 2" strips and several narrow 6" strips of foil paper and curl them over a scissor blade. Glue the short strips to the head and the long strips to the tail.

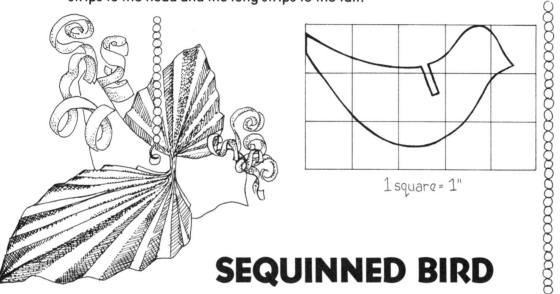

1 square = 1"

SEQUINNED BIRD

Materials: Posterboard or 3- or 4-ply Bristol board; metallic foil paper; sequins.

Using the graphs as guides, cut a bird out of posterboard and 4 feathers from foil paper. Stack the feathers and cut fringes in the sides, without cutting too close to the center lines. Fold each feather in half. Make 2 pairs of feathers by slipping 1 feather into another and gluing at the base. Glue each pair to the back of the bird. Decorate the bird with sequins.

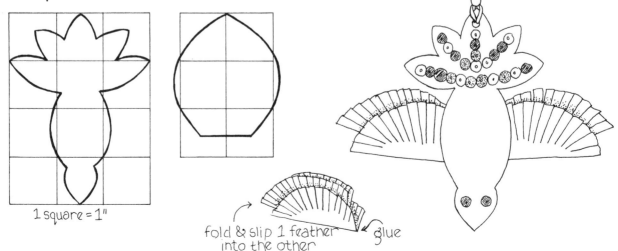

1 square = 1"

fold & slip 1 feather into the other

glue

FRINGED TREE

Materials: Construction paper; sequins or scraps of colored papers.

Using the graphs as guides, cut 2 of each tree part and 1 trunk. (NOTE: If you are making more than 1 tree, make re-usable scrap paper patterns of the parts.) Snip a fringe in each part and curl the fringes around a pencil. Glue all the parts together, tucking the trunk between the 2 largest parts. Decorate both sides of the tree with sequins or with circles cut out of scraps.

1 square = 1"

TISSUE PAPER WREATH WITH BOW

Materials: Tissue paper—2 or 3 colors for the wreath and 1 for the bow.

Bow: Cut a rectangle with pinked ends and pinch tightly at the center. Wind a narrow 3" long strip of tissue around the center and glue the end. Glue 4 or 5 narrow tissue streamers to the back of the bow. Curl 2 or 3 of the streamers over a scissor blade.

Wreath: Cut 3 strips of tissue, each about 20" long and 3" wide. Crush each strip down the length, braid the strips together and glue the ends. Keeping the braid flat, form into a circle and glue 1 end to the other. Glue the bow over the joined ends.

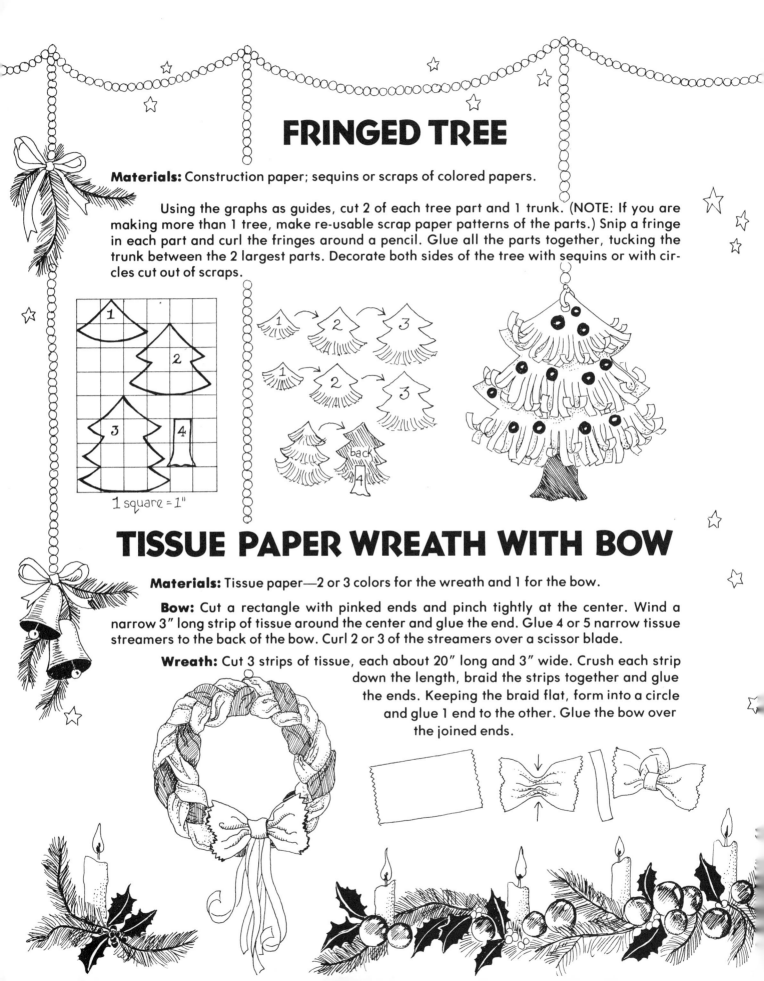

MEXICAN STAR WITH STREAMERS

Materials: Posterboard; any kind of colored paper; tissue paper.

Cut parts 1 and 3 out of colored paper as shown; cut parts 2 and 4 out of poster-board as shown. Glue the parts together in order—1 on 2, 2 on 3, 3 on 4. Cut about 20 narrow tissue strips for streamers, the more colors the better. Glue 6 or 7 streamers to the back of each of 3 points.

THREE-COLOR STAR

Materials: Thin, easily creased paper like origami paper, flint paper, giftwrap, or bond paper.

Cut 3 squares of the same size in 3 different colors. Pleat each square diagonally. Fasten the pleated squares together with a narrow paper strip wound tightly around the centers and glued. Fan out the 6 sections, dab glue on adjoining pleats, and clip together with paper clips until the glue is dry.

glue & clip

CORNUCOPIAS

Materials: Construction paper; decorative materials like doilies, gummed stickers, cut-out pictures, ribbon, spangles.

Start with a 9" x 12" piece of construction paper. Bring up 1 corner and then the other corner to make a cone. Wrap the paper almost double to keep the cone narrow and pull up gently on the inside corner to tighten the point. Hold the cone firmly while you glue the inside and outside edges. Cut the top edge in any of the ways shown and trim with the decorative materials. Glue on a handle to make a cornucopia into a basket.

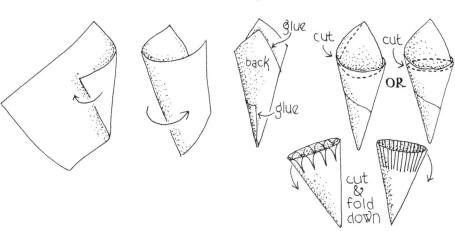

THREE-DIMENSIONAL HEARTS, STARS, AND OTHER SHAPES

Materials: Scrap paper for making a pattern; construction paper, 1- or 2-ply Bristol board, bond paper, metallic paper, Aurora paper, or other similar paper.

On scrap paper draw the shape you choose, divide it in half, and cut this pattern out. Outline the pattern 4 times on folded construction or other paper to make 4 identical folded shapes. Cut out each shape through both layers. Glue the shapes together as shown.

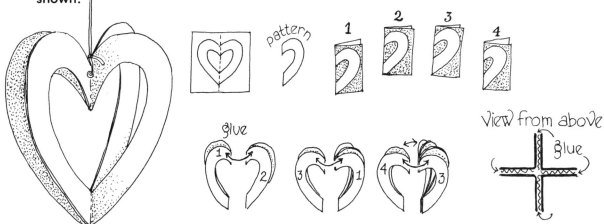

LACY HEART WITH RIBBON STREAMERS

Materials: Construction or other colored paper; doilies; ribbon (NOTE: Inexpensive ribbed giftwrapping ribbon is best for this ornament because it can be curled.)

Cut 2 identical hearts. On 1 heart glue a lacy border made of parts cut from doilies. At the point of the same heart glue 4 or 5 ribbon streamers curled over a scissor blade. Glue the second heart over the first and decorate with cut-paper flowers, hearts, leaves, bows, birds.

1st heart

2nd heart

HEART BASKET

Materials: Construction or other colored paper.

Cut 2 identical hearts. Outline 1 of the hearts on a piece of contrasting paper. Cut out the contrasting heart ¾ " outside the pencil line. Snip a fringe in the edge of the contrasting heart, cutting slightly past the pencil line. Glue 1 of the 2 identical hearts to the fringed heart, positioning it on the pencil line. Put glue along the lower edge of the remaining heart and press it into position on the other side of the fringed heart. Allow the glue to dry. Glue a handle to the inside front and back of the basket. Fill the basket with goodies.

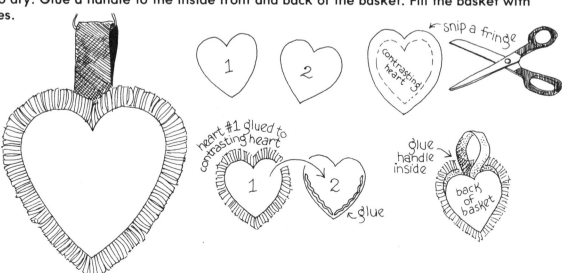

61

CHINESE LANTERN

Materials: Scrap paper for making a pattern; posterboard; tissue paper.

Make a pattern as shown and use it to draw the lantern shape on posterboard. The additional ½ " tab you see will be used to glue the lantern together.

Cut out the lantern and score the indicated lines with a mat knife or single-edge razor blade. Cut a design out of each panel of the lantern, being careful not to cut as far as any of the scored lines or the top or bottom edges. Back each panel with a different color of tissue paper. Let the glue dry.

Fold the lantern into shape along the scored lines and glue the tab inside the first panel. Clip the tab with clothespins or paper clips while the glue dries. Glue long, narrow tissue paper streamers to the 8 corners of the lantern and curl some of the streamers over a scissor blade. Hang the lantern as shown.

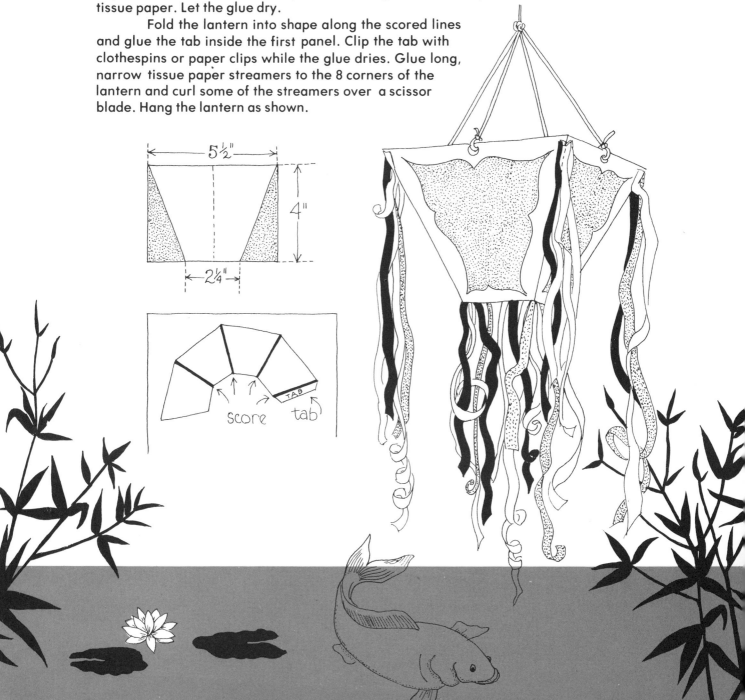

RAINBOW FISH

Materials: 7 or 8 colors of construction paper.

Using the graphs as guides, cut 2 identical heads and 1 of each of the other 6 parts. NOTE: Each of the 6 parts is cut from a <u>folded</u> piece of construction paper. The tail is made of 2 half-circles. Slip the parts into each other in order and glue, with the head and tail glued on last. Glue on small cut-paper circles for eyes.

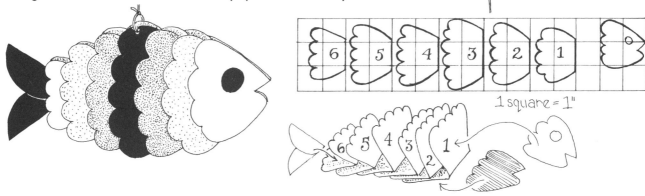

1 square = 1"

WOVEN FISH

Materials: Construction paper, Aurora paper, or other colored paper.

Cut 2 long, narrow strips of paper. Carefully follow the steps in the drawings to weave the fish. When the fish is complete, snip off the tails and fins at steep angles. Glue on sequins for eyes.

NOTE: When working with paper colored on 1 side only, like Aurora or flint paper, begin step 1 with the colors facing away from you.

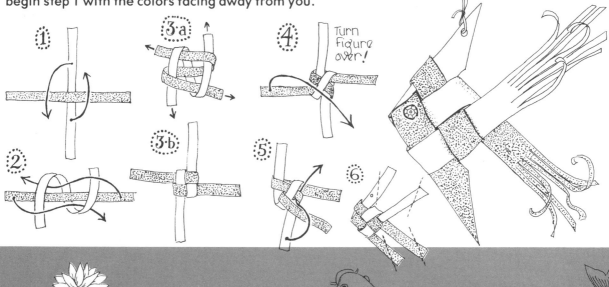

BUTTERFLY

Materials: Thin, easily creased paper like origami paper, flint paper, giftwrap, or bond paper.

Cut 2 squares, 1 larger than the other. Pleat each square diagonally. Fasten the pleated squares together with a narrow paper strip, wound tightly around the centers and glued. For decoration, snip bits out of the folds, as shown. Fan out the wings and glue them together, clipping with paper clips, bulldog clips, or clothespins until the glue is dry.

fasten

fan out, glue & clip

PARASOL

Materials: Construction paper or similar paper; half of a pipe cleaner for each parasol; sequins (optional).

Cut a construction paper circle 5" in diameter. Pencil it off into 8 equal wedges and cut the edge into scallops, 2 scallops per wedge. Decorate with cut-paper flowers and leaves and a sequin or 2. Cut along 1 pencil line to the center, apply some glue, and overlap 1 scallop. Poke a small hole in the point. Push the tip of half a pipe cleaner through the hole and fold the tip over so it won't slip out. Bend the other end of the pipe cleaner into a handle. Apply a bit of glue to the pipe cleaner where it touches the point; this will keep the paper shade from wobbling. Rest the parasol in a tall glass while the glue dries.

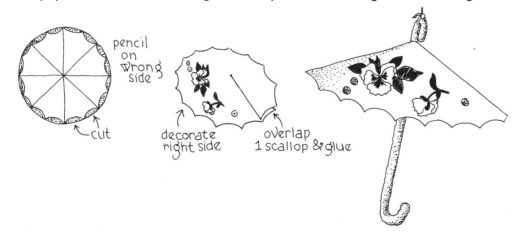

pencil on wrong side

cut

decorate right side

overlap 1 scallop & glue

PARTY DECORATIONS

MASKS TOYS + SILLY HATS

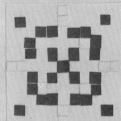

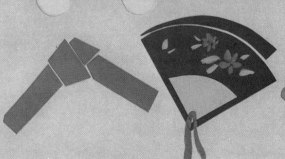

NOTES

CARDS

INVITATIONS

ORIGAMI CRANE

The crane is the most popular of all traditional origami figures. Follow the drawings step by step, folding as precisely as you can. Work with a large square, between 7" and 9".

Materials: Origami paper or other thin paper like flint paper or giftwrap.

1. Fold in half.

2. Crease in half again. Unfold.

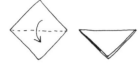

3. Open 1 corner and bring the point down. Crease the paper.

4. Turn the paper over and repeat step 3 on the other corner.

5. Crease on 1 side as shown and unfold. Turn the paper over.

turn over & repeat on other side

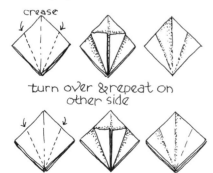

6. Crease the top and unfold. Lift the point as shown and bring the sides in. Crease neatly.

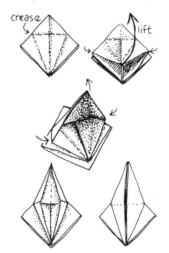

7. Turn the figure over and repeat step 6.

8. Fold the sides in to the center. Turn the figure over and repeat.

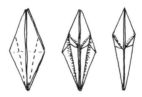

9. Crease each side as shown and unfold. Now refold both sides, inverting the folds between the front and back.

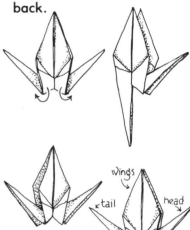

10. Fold the head and wings down.

11. Hold the crane by the wings with the underside toward you. Blow sharply into the small hole to puff out the crane's body.

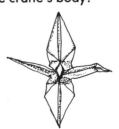

65

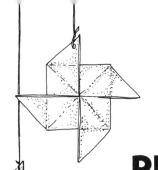
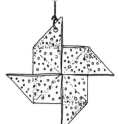

ORIGAMI
PINWHEEL AND STARFLOWER

Begin with a 6″ to 9″ square.

Materials: Origami paper or other thin paper like flint paper or giftwrap.

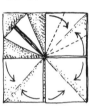

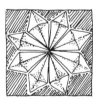

Pinwheel

1. Fold the sides to the center. Fold in half.

2. Fold the front up in half. Crease as shown and unfold.

3. Pull out the inner corners.

4. Turn the figure over and repeat steps 2 and 3.

5. The figure looks like this now.

Open it flat to look like this.

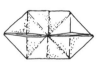

6. Fold 1 point up and 1 point down.

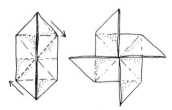

7. Tack each of the 4 parts down with dabs of glue. This is the completed pinwheel.

Starflower

To make the starflower, first do steps 1 through 6 of the pinwheel and then proceed to step 7 of the starflower.

7. Open each part and bring the point to the center.

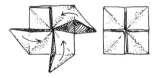

8. Fold the edges of each of the quarters into the middle.

9. Crease the little corners as shown. Unfold and open out each little part.

opened out

10. Carefully cut away the shaded areas. Do not snip off any of the points.

11. With dabs of glue, tack down the points in the center. If desired, decorate with a sequin or a cut-out glued over the center.

6. PARTY DECORATIONS

When I was in the ninth grade, I volunteered to be head of the Decorating Committee for the Freshman Prom. My credentials included decorations for half a dozen of my own birthday parties and straight A's in art. I got the job.

The freshman class, in support of what we considered a brilliantly original idea, voted for Neptune's Night Spot as the prom theme. The Decorating Committee proceeded to plan accordingly. We collected every shell in Tenafly, New Jersey. We borrowed hunks of coral. We bought out the stores of every package of blue and green crepe paper in sight.

The moment I remember best, my moment of glory, was when a pair of huge, filthy volleyball nets which had been lashed to various rings and hoops around the gym were slowly hoisted into position half way to the ceiling, dripping with sea sponges, streamers, and other junk, while dozens of chaperoning mothers and spectators watched open-mouthed. No doubt, they were seized with horror at the sheer madness of airborne volleyball nets that might fall down mid-Prom and trap hundreds of terrified ninth graders. Fortunately, the net stayed put and my interior decorating career was launched.

Here are paper decorations for 4 parties: Mexican, Valentine's Day, Japanese, and birthday parties. The Mexican and Japanese decorations are all-purpose decorating schemes; use them for any adult or children's party. The Mexican decorations are especially nice for a Christmas party since they feature a piñata, the traditional Mexican Christmas party treat. The Valentine's Day party decorations are strictly for February 14, my favorite holiday. The birthday party decorations are adaptable to any holiday. Simply change the cut-out message from HAPPY BIRTHDAY to HAPPY HALLOWEEN or HAPPY HANUKKAH or whatever you like and change a few of the hanging decorations to the appropriate holiday symbols—pumpkins, Christmas trees, flags, turkeys, shamrocks.

How to make strings of hanging decorations

All 4 party plans feature paper decorations that float in the air, hanging from strings that extend from 1 part of the room to another. The string (cotton wrapping string, crochet cotton like Speed-Cro-Sheen, or other sturdy thin string) is tied at each end to some stationary object. Except for the Mexican banners and streamers, all the strings of hanging decorations are made in basically the same way.

1. Measure the distance to be covered by the string in the air.

The distance is from 1 stationary object in the party room to another stationary object in the same room. This object can be anything 7' or higher in the air; the possibilities are limited only by what's available in the party room—curtain rod, light fixture, nail in the wall, hook in the ceiling (like the ones for hanging plants), bookshelf bracket, pole of an etagère or room divider, door hinge, or even a stairway bannister or baluster.

Tie string taut from 1 chosen object to the other, allow an extra foot or 2, and cut the string. Untie the string.

2. Now tie the measured string across the room at about waist level, from the back of a chair to the doorknob or similar place, so you can work on the decorations easily, saving yourself sore arm muscles.

3. Cut out the shapes—lanterns, hearts, flowers, or whatever is called for—and decorate them as necessary. With a paper punch, make a hole in the top of each shape.

4. Cut a 10" piece of thin string for each shape. Tie it to the shape at the punched hole.

5. Tie all shapes to the main string, spacing them attractively.

6. Untie the main string from the chair and doorknob and retie it securely to the same objects used for measuring in step 1. This is easier if you have a helper to hold 1 end of the main string while you are climbing on the stepladder to tie the first end.

Repeat this whole process to make each string of hanging decorations.

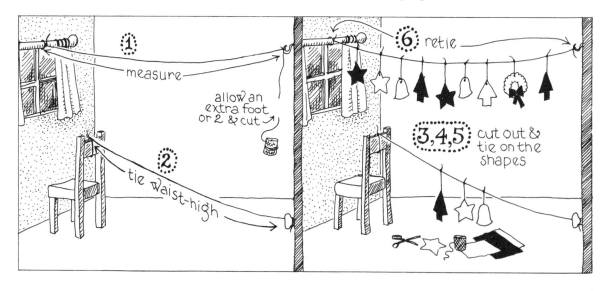

MEXICAN DECORATIONS

Most Mexican folk art is brightly colored and boldly patterned, but delicate tissue paper banners, streamers, and garlands are traditionally white and pale pastels. Save the fiesta red, tropical green, and sunshine yellow for the bouquets of crepe paper flowers, the Mexican stars, and the papier maché piñatas.

Banners and Streamers

Materials: Tissue paper—buy economy packages of 20" x 30" sheets in white or pastels.

To make banners, first enlarge the graph onto a piece of heavy paper and draw the pattern square by square. Cut out the pattern. Cut 4 banners at a time: Fold 2 sheets of tissue in half, in quarters, and then eighths as shown; place the straight lines of the pattern on the folds of the tissue; outline the pattern and remove it; cut out the banners through all layers. Do <u>not</u> cut off any folds. Separate into 4 folded banners.

To make streamers, first stack 2 or 3 whole sheets of tissue. Fold in half and then in quarters. Cut 1"-wide strips. Separate into individual folded streamers.

Tie strings across the party room as described in step 1 on page 68. Each folded banner or streamer is draped over the string with no other fastening. You won't know exactly how many banners and streamers you need, so just cut several to start and make more as you go. Try different combinations: banners separated by 4 or 5 streamers; whole strings of streamers; white banners with pastel streamers.

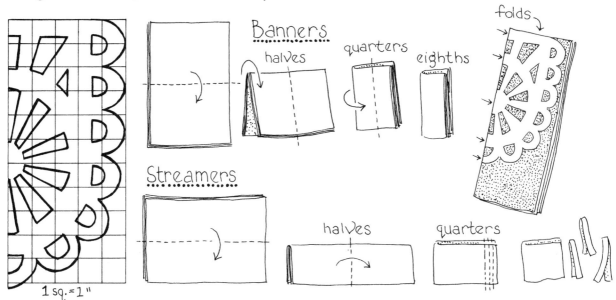

Mexican Star with Streamers

Instructions for making the Mexican star are on page 59 in Chapter 5, Hanging Ornaments. Hang or tape a Mexican star wherever banners, streamers, or garlands meet the walls.

Flower-and-Straw Garlands

Materials: Pastel-colored paper drinking straws; white tissue paper; heavy-duty thread and large needle.

Stack a dozen sheets of tissue and cut into approximately 2 ½" squares. Cut each stack of a dozen squares into circles and then snip petals to make flowers.

Thread the needle and tie a knot near the needle as shown. Do not cut the thread; this allows you to make as long a garland as you like. Thread a 2" section of paper straw onto the needle and push it down a few feet. Then thread 4 tissue flowers and a whole straw. Continue alternating groups of 4 flowers and whole straws, pushing them further and further along the thread, until the garland is the desired length. Thread another 2" piece of straw and secure it by looping the thread around several times, tying off, and cutting the thread. Go back to the beginning of the garland and secure the first short straw.

Drape garlands around the walls, across the room, over the doorways and windows.

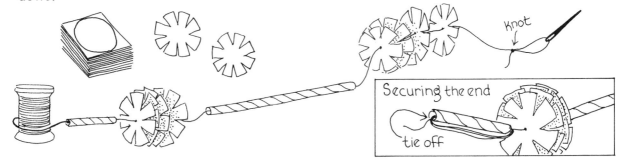

Crepe Paper Flowers

Make bunches of large paper flowers from Chapter 4. Put the bouquets in pottery jars, baskets, or terra-cotta flowerpots.

Papier Maché Piñata

A piñata is made of papier maché or earthenware molded to look like an animal or geometric shape. It is decorated with colorful tissue paper and filled with candy, toys, and small gifts. After the piñata is suspended from the ceiling, children take turns playing the piñata game: Each child is blindfolded, whirled around 3 times, and given 3 tries to smash the piñata with a broomstick. Breaking the piñata and catching the goodies are the most exciting moments for children at a Mexican Christmas party. If you prefer, piñatas may be hung up as decorations without being filled.

Materials: Newspaper torn into scraps about 2″ square; flour and water to make paste; 1 tube of acrylic paint and a paint brush; spherical balloon; Vaseline; empty flowerpot; assorted colors of tissue paper.

In a bowl, mix 1 cup of flour plus enough water to make a paste the consistency of pancake batter. Blow up the balloon, tie it off, and rub the surface with a thin coat of Vaseline. Balance the balloon, tied end down, in the flowerpot.

Dip pieces of newspaper in the paste and apply them 1 by 1 to the balloon, overlapping and smoothing each piece as you apply it. Cover the balloon completely with 1 layer of newspaper; the only part that should not be covered is the part of the balloon resting out of sight in the flowerpot. Apply 2 more layers of newspaper.

Let the papier maché dry completely. This may take 24 hours or more. Speed up the process if necessary by putting the piñata in a warm oven with the heat turned off. When the piñata is completely dry, pop the balloon and remove it. Rub the inside of the piñata with a soft rag to clean off any Vaseline residue. Let the piñata dry for another 24 hours.

Paint the piñata with 2 coats of acrylic paint, allowing each coat to dry thoroughly. Decorate the piñata with bands of fringed tissue paper strips and bands of crumpled squares of tissue.

Fringed strips: Cut strips of tissue 2″ high and 6″ long. Snip a 1 ½″ fringe in each strip and carefully curl the fringes over a scissor blade. Glue the strips to the piñata, overlapping them, working up from the closed end.

Crumpled squares: Cut 2″ squares of tissue and crumple each one into a ball. Glue them to the piñata in bands as shown.

Glue curled tissue paper streamers to the bottom of the piñata. Use a nail to make 3 holes around the rim and tie string as shown.

VALENTINE DECORATIONS

Revel in hearts and flowers. Make most of them in red, white, and pale pink paper, (the traditional valentine colors), but spike the color scheme with touches of lavender, light blue, shocking pink, aqua, bright green, and pale yellow.

Hearts-on-a-String

String hearts up according to the general directions in the introduction, page 68. Make as many hearts as you need to fill the strings generously. NOTE: The Lacy Heart with Streamers (page 61), Three-Dimensional Heart (page 60), and the Heart Basket (page 61) may also be enlarged to become Hearts-on-a-String.

Materials: Construction paper and other colored papers; thin string or crochet cotton (pearl cotton or Knit-Cro-Sheen, available in the 5-and-10).

Graduated hearts: Cut 3 hearts in graduated sizes and snip out the centers. Dab glue on the hearts and lay a piece of thin string over the glue as shown. Let the glue dry.

Large and small hearts: Cut 1 large heart (using 1 sheet of construction paper) and 3 small ones. Punch holes in the hearts and tie them together as shown.

Heart made of strips: Cut half a sheet of construction paper into 4 strips. Glue the 4 strips together, with a length of string sandwiched between the middle strips as shown in the drawing. Secure with paper clips while the glue dries. Curve the strips around, glue them in place, and clip while they dry.

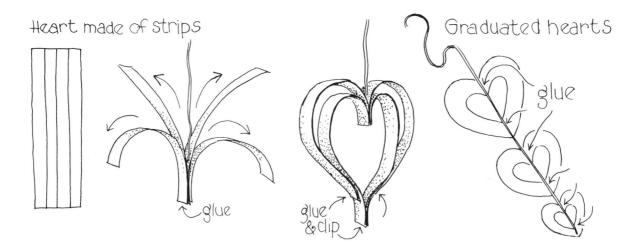

Heart made of strips

glue

glue & clip

Graduated hearts

glue

Valentine Wall Display

If Scotch or masking tape won't damage your walls, put up a wall display of valentine mementoes—cut-paper hearts in different sizes, cupids enlarged onto colored paper from the graph shown here, valentine cards you have saved, cards your friends bring to the party, lacy valentines you make yourself, accordian-folded garlands. Attach each piece to the wall with loops of tape.

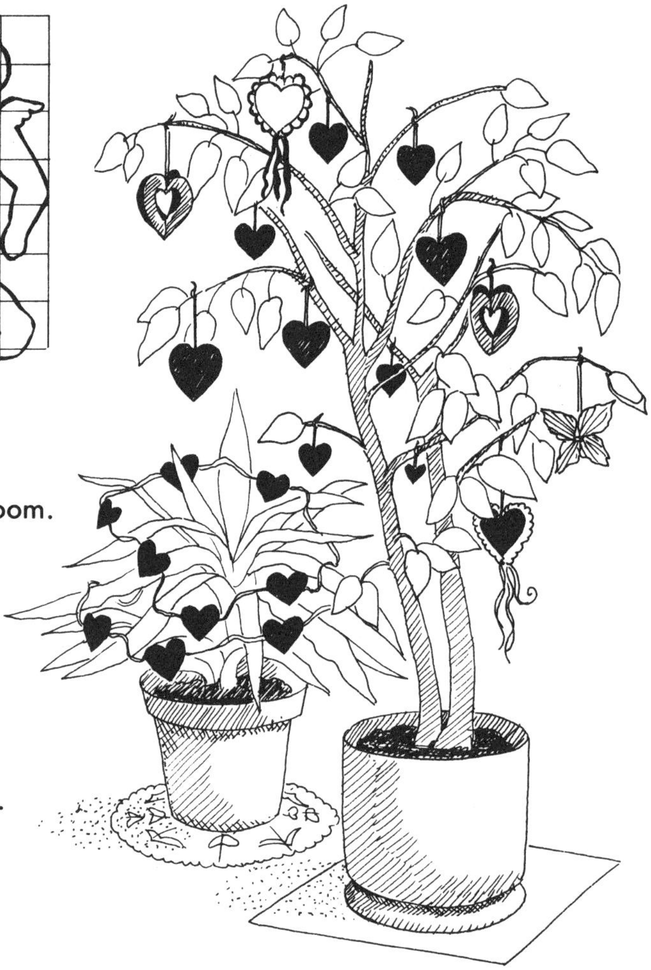

Valentine Garden

Bring all your houseplants into the party room. Borrow some extras if you don't have very many. Decorate the large plants with small hanging ornaments like the Three-Dimensional Heart (page 60), Butterfly (page 64), or plain hearts cut from colored and metallic papers. Decorate the smaller plants with garlands of hearts: Cut dozens of pairs of small hearts from colored paper; glue pairs of the hearts together along a string, sandwiching the string between the hearts.

Flowers

Make bowls of red, pink, and white paper flowers with plenty of green leaves (see Chapter 4, Flowers). Glue paper hearts to the ends of real branches or thin dowels—like lollipops—and tuck them into the bouquets.

Mats and Doilies

Bowls of flowers and plates of food can sit on simple cut-paper doilies and mats. Read about single-fold paper-cutting on page 27 and triple-fold paper-cutting on page 36. Invent your own designs, using the drawings for ideas.

JAPANESE DECORATIONS

For this party plan, I have borrowed some traditional Japanese ideas on papercraft and festival decorations. A suggestion on color: Colors used in the decorations for Japanese celebrations are always in keeping with the festival spirit—scarlet, turquoise blue, bright yellow, violet, pink, leaf green, metallic gold and silver.

Lanterns, Flowers, Fans, and Streamers

Read the general instructions for making strings of hanging decorations (page 68). Put up several strings of hanging lanterns of different shapes and colors, several strings of flowers, fans, or streamers, and several strings that mix all the designs.

Materials: Construction paper and other colored and metallic papers; tissue paper; spangles.

Lantern: Each lantern consists of a long, narrow rectangle sandwiched with glue between a front and a back. Front and back may be decorated with paper cut-outs.

Flowers: To make a flower pattern, enlarge the graph onto heavy paper and draw the flower square by square. Cut out the pattern and outline it on colored paper. Cut out each outlined flower and decorate with tissue paper streamers and spangles or with smaller cut-paper flowers and dangling circles.

Fan: Use a compass to draw the rounded edge. Tie on dangling flowers or circles.

Streamer #1: Cut 5 rectangles, each 3 ½ ″ x 4 ½ ″, and glue them together with the edges overlapping as shown.

Streamer #2: Cut 1″ x 9″ rectangles and hang them alone or in combination with other shapes.

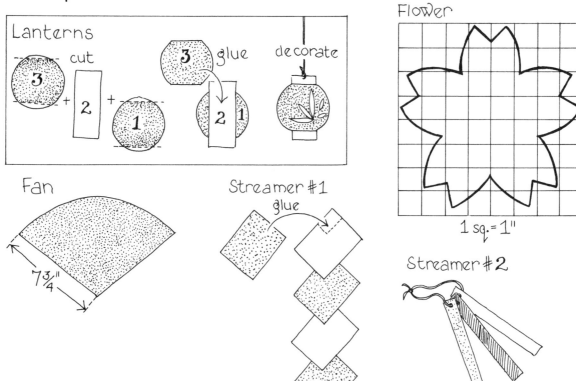

Doorway Decoration

In every doorway, taped to the doorframe, hang vertical rows of small flowers with streamers. Use the graph as a guide for cutting out flowers.

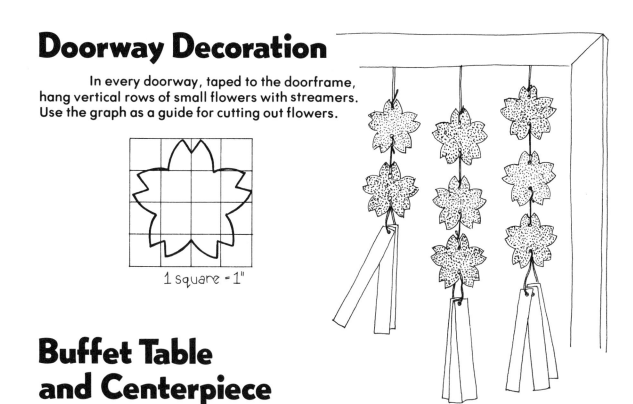

1 square = 1"

Buffet Table and Centerpiece

Include some origami figures in a centerpiece of plants, flowers, or fruit. For example, perch several small origami cranes among the leaves of a plant. Suspend origami star-flowers, pinwheels, and cranes above the buffet table, either from the ceiling or from the light fixture. Make origami boxes for nuts and candy. Instructions for the pinwheel and starflower are on page 66, for the crane on page 65, and for the boxes on pages 116 and 117.

Invitations

Cut invitations in the shape of fans or lanterns, using folded sheets of paper. You might prefer to buy small folded notes with matching envelopes and decorate them with cut-outs of fans or lanterns. See page 123 and page 118 for general instructions on making the invitations.

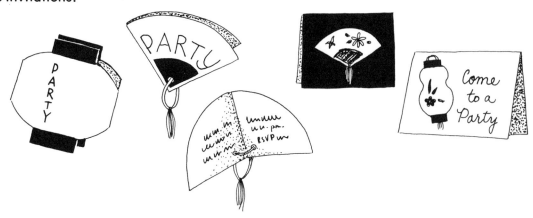

BIRTHDAY PARTY DECORATIONS

Try these fast and easy decorations for any birthday party—adult's or child's—or bend the basic idea to fit any kind of holiday party. For example, if you want to change birthday decorations to Christmas decorations, first change the shape of the invitations from wedges of birthday cake to wreaths or Santas. Next, change some of the hanging shapes to appropriate symbols, like Christmas trees, candy canes, and bells. Finally, rewrite the hanging-letter message to read MERRY CHRISTMAS and make the crepe paper streamers red, green, and white.

Strings of Geometric Shapes

Materials: Construction paper; packages of narrow paper streamers available in the 5-and-10.

Hang strings of stars, diamonds, circles, and triangles, using the method described in the introduction on page 68. Cut 1 geometric shape from each sheet of brightly colored construction paper. Unfurl the streamers and toss them over the strings.

Strings of Letters

Materials: Construction paper; Scotch or masking tape.

Spell out HAPPY BIRTHDAY (or any other message) across the room in foot-high capital letters. Cut each letter from a sheet of 9" x 12" construction paper. Draw the letter first, making it fill the sheet.

Measure the main string and tie it across the room at waist level (see instructions on page 68 in the introduction). Fold over the top of each letter about ½". Position the letters in order in the center section of the string. Remove each letter one at a time and dab a little glue inside the fold. Replace each letter in position and tape it on the back. Add some geometric shapes and hang the string in position as described in the introduction.

Crepe Paper Streamers

Supplement the decorations with store-bought crepe paper streamers. Tape streamers from wall to wall, twisting them for a festive look. Tape them fairly high up because crepe paper stretches and tends to sag. Gaffer tape, a strong tape used by electricians, is the best to use; buy it in a hardware store. (NOTE: If you are concerned about the effect of the tape on your walls, make a patch test by leaving a small piece of tape stuck for a few hours on an unnoticeable part of the wall. Pull it off gently and examine the wall.)

Dip-in-Dye Table Mats and Place Mats

Cut tableau paper to the desired sizes for place mats or table mats. Dye according to the instructions for dip-in-dye decorating on page 21 in Chapter 2.

Invitations

Make invitations in the shape of wedges of birthday cake or in some other shape if you are giving a different kind of party—boats or trains for a bon voyage party, Christmas trees for a Christmas party, jack-o'-lanterns for Halloween. Read the general instructions on page 123.

Favors

For a sit-down dinner, make a basket for each guest (Chapter 9). Fill the baskets with nuts, candies, and mints.

For a small party, make a simple favor for each guest: tissue or crepe paper flower (Chapter 4); small book (Chapter 7); cut-paper doily mounted on pretty paper (Chapter 3); mask or silly hat (Chapter 8); finger puppet for a child (Chapter 8).

7. BOOKS

A book is a lasting and permanent thing. Until my sophomore year as an art student, I was sure that only a machine could make a real book, with binding and end-papers and pages that wouldn't fall out. But during that year, I learned that anyone can make a beautiful book. It happened when a special teacher we called the Book Lady came to the campus and spent a week showing us exactly how to do it. Bookbinding equipment was brought in, pots of glue boiled, and the general atmosphere was like an alchemist's laboratory. At the end of the week, each student had made several books with blank pages which were then covered with poetry written out in newly-learned calligraphy and illustrated with drawings and paintings.

Since then, I have learned to make books in ways that are simple and require no special equipment, using the same materials that are used for every other kind of paper project. When you try these methods and make books of your own, the best part is that you can fill the blank pages with anything that pleases you: drawings, cartoons, clippings, recipes, poetry, photographs, autographs, stamp collections, travel mementoes, picture postcards, love letters, autumn leaves, or spring flowers.

What's in a book

Most books are made up of a front cover and a back cover with decorative paper covering them on the outside and lining them on the inside, blank pages, and occasionally, endpapers (which are bound into the book between the cover and the pages). All these parts can be confusing to a beginner, so the instructions for making each book in this chapter are very specific. Once you have made a book following my directions, you will be prepared to try out book design ideas on your own — perhaps a book that is very large or small, one that is long and narrow or perfectly square, or one that is made with your own choice of papers. In the course of making books from my designs or your own, you will need to know the information that follows on the next few pages.

About measuring

Measurements must be accurate. This ensures that the parts of the finished book will fit together in perfect alignment. If you are careless, the book will be lopsided and you will be unhappy with the results.

How to cut with a mat knife or single-edge razor blade

Safe, clean cutting of heavy papers and boards is essential. Follow these rules to cut correctly.

1. Start with the right equipment.

Cover the worktable with a cutting surface like a large piece of chipboard (see page 13 for further information). Any ruler will do for measuring but use a metal straight edge (described on page 12) when cutting. You must have either a mat knife and a generous supply of mat knife blades or just a generous supply of single-edge razor blades. Always start cutting with a new blade. When it dulls, turn the blade around and use the opposite corner; when that dulls, wrap the dulled edge in masking tape and throw it away. A dull blade is a dangerous blade — it won't grip the paper or board and therefore it can slip out of control.

2. Measure correctly and mark the cutting line with pencil. Lay a metal straight edge on the pencil line, rest a blade securely against the straight edge, and draw the blade over the paper or board with long, firm, steady strokes.

Stand up while you are cutting and keep your body out of the path of the blade. Rest your hand firmly on the metal straight edge to keep it steady and unmoving while you draw the blade along with the other hand. The metal straight edge acts as a guide for the blade; the blade must be touching the straight edge at all times while cutting. Use firm — not heavy — pressure on the blade. Pressing too heavily may send the blade swerving. Make repeated strokes and have patience; cutting is accomplished not by making 3 heavy-handed strokes, but by making 10 to 15 light, firm ones. WARNING: Never do knife or blade cutting when you are tired and shaky.

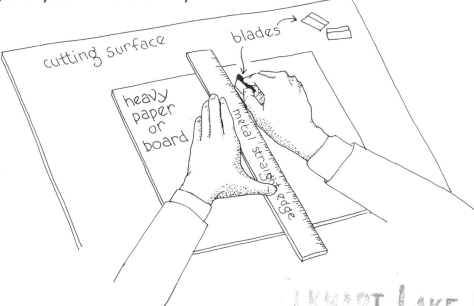

About ironing

Wrinkled or creased papers should be ironed before being used in making a book. Set a dry iron at the lowest heat, spread the paper on the ironing board, and iron gently. If wrinkles don't come out, increase the heat gradually until the paper irons flat.

About buckling

When glue is applied to 1 side of the board or paper, the wetness causes mild or extreme buckling. This buckling may worry you, especially when you are working on the covers of a book. When this happens, remind yourself that when you apply glue to the other side of each board, it buckles in the opposite direction and flattens out naturally. Any slight curve that remains can be pressed out by stacking heavy books on the boards.

Decorating any finished book

Decorating the outside or inside of the front or back covers can enhance the beauty of a book. Here are a few suggestions for decorations.

◆ Decorate with carefully cut out decoupage prints, parts of doilies, pictures cut from gardening catalogues, greeting cards, or giftwrap. Brush slightly diluted glue sparingly but completely on the back, press the picture in position, and wipe off any excess glue.

◆ Cut letters from colored papers or from newspapers and magazines. Use the letters to label the book or, if you are giving the book as a gift, to spell out a name and date on the inside of the book.

◆ Take some ideas from the chapter on paper-cutting, pages 26 to 37.

 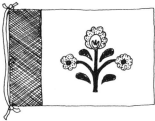  

◆ Glue on a cut-paper quilt pattern or a mosaic made of small squares of construction paper. Check out the ideas described on pages 120 and 119.

Points to remember
when you design your own book

1. When redesigning the size or shape of a book from this chapter, remember to accommodate the new dimensions by changing the measurements of the covering paper, lining paper, pages, and all other parts of the book.

2. For covering the outside of the front and back boards, I have had the most success with fibrous papers that give or stretch a little when they are damp from glue — for example, heavy rice papers, tableau paper (which can be decorated by the dip-in-dye technique described on page 21), heavy charcoal and pastel papers, Japanese and other imported giftwraps. The crisper papers like ordinary giftwrap, flint paper, and metallic paper can be tricky because they tend to wrinkle. Thin papers like tissue and delicate rice paper work well, but you should be aware that the color of the boards will be faintly revealed through the partial transparency of the paper.

Some papers are definitely unsuitable for covering: construction paper, crepe paper, newsprint, tracing paper, and shelf paper.

3. When you are picking a paper for lining the inside of the front and back covers, choose just about anything but crepe paper. Linings don't have to withstand stress the way covering papers do, so the possibilities are wider. Choose on the basis of interest, originality, and appropriateness rather than pure practicality.

LOOSE-LEAF BOOK

Thin rice paper covers and mutes the colored mat boards that form the front and back of this book. The pages are tied rather than bound permanently into the book — an unusual kind of Japanese binding that allows you to change the pages whenever you like. Use the book horizontally or vertically.

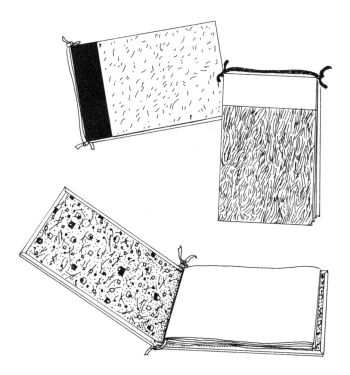

Materials: 2 pieces of single thick mat board, each 7" x 10", colored on 1 or both sides, for the front and back covers; 1 strip of bond paper, 7" x 1 3/8"; 1 strip of thin white cotton cloth, 7" x 1 3/8"; 1 piece of thin rice paper, 9" x 22", for covering the boards; 1 strip of metallic paper, 9" x 4 ½", for the decorative spine; 1 piece of patterned paper (may be Japanese printed paper, giftwrap, or a paper you have patterned yourself using a technique from Chapter 2), 6 ¾" x 20", for lining the boards; 2 pieces of pretty cord or cotton string, each 12" long, for the binding; 10 pieces of bond paper or thin charcoal paper, each piece 6 ¾" x 20", for the pages.

1. Join the front and back covers together with the bond paper strip.

Brush slightly diluted glue along 1 short edge of the outside of 1 board. (NOTE: If the mat board is colored on 1 side only, be sure that colored side is designated as the outside.) Overlap the bond paper strip ½" on the gluey edge and smooth it out. Turn the board and strip over and butt them against a ruler. Apply glue to 1 short edge of the outside of the other board and position it glue-side-down on the paper strip, 3/8" away from the first board, butted against the

ruler. Allow to dry. NOTE: Butting the boards against the ruler keeps the boards even and allows you to measure 3/8" at the same time.

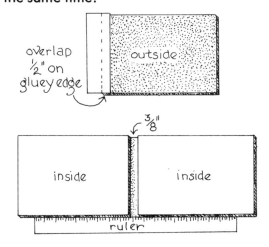

2. Glue the cotton strip to the boards.

Brush slightly diluted glue along the short edges of the inside of the boards and onto the paper between the boards. Center and smooth the cotton strip over the glue, pressing it into the valley between the boards so the cloth adheres to the paper strip. Let it dry.

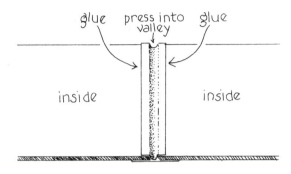

3. Cover the joined boards with the rice paper.

Center the joined boards on the rice paper, with the outside (colored side) of the boards touching the rice paper. Outline the boards with pencil. Remove the boards and clip the corners of the rice paper.

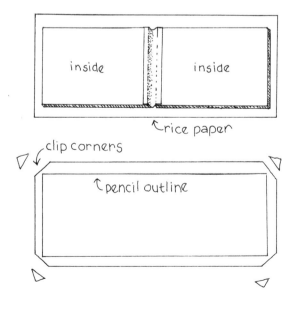

With a large brush, apply slightly diluted glue to the outside of the boards right to the edges and position them glue-side-down on the rice paper, within the pencil outline. Immediately turn the boards and paper over and smooth out the rice paper.

Turn the boards back to the inside and brush glue on the long edges. Bring the rice paper up and smooth it over the glue, pressing the paper into the valley between the boards. Brush glue along the short edges and under the paper at the corners of the boards. Make neat corners as shown, bring the rice paper up, and smooth it over the glue.

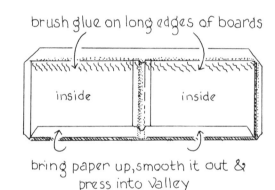

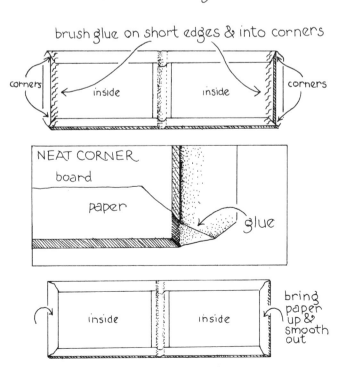

4. Glue the decorative spine to the outside of the boards.

With pencil, mark a line down the center of the wrong side of the spine paper. Brush slightly diluted glue on the wrong side. Center the covered boards over the spine and press the boards down on the spine. Turn the boards over and smooth out the spine paper. Turn back to the inside and bring the ends of the spine around to the inside of the boards, smoothing them down. With a small brush, glue down any loose corners and edges.

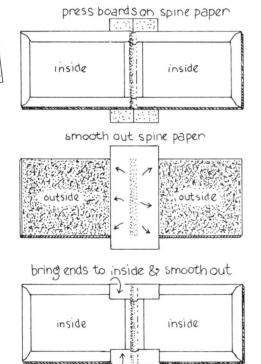

Set the spine by folding the book along the spine, aligning the corners of the boards, and flattening out the curve of the spine with your finger.

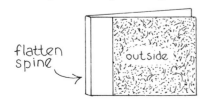

5. Glue the lining paper to the inside of the boards.

With a large brush, apply slightly diluted glue to the inside of the boards almost to the edges. Center the lining paper carefully over the glue. Smooth down the lining paper, pressing it into the center valley between the boards.

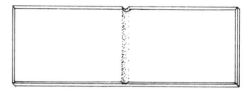

With a small brush, glue down any loose edges and corners. Wipe off excess glue with a damp (not wet) paper towel. Leave the unfinished book open and stack heavy books on each of the boards to flatten them while they dry.

6. Prepare the pages and insert them into the book.

Stack the 10 pages and fold them in half. Measure 9 ½ " from the fold and trim off excess paper with a mat knife or single-edge razor blade.

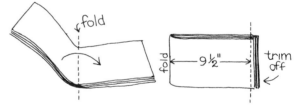

Place 1 of the 12" cords inside the middle page along the fold and put the pages in the book. Tie the other 12" cord to the first cord at top and bottom. Tie securely with triple knots and dab a bit of glue on the last knot. Clip off the excess cord.

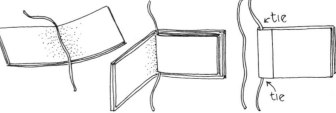

ALBUM-STYLE BOOK

In this familiar style of the family photo album, the front and back boards are not joined. Each is covered and lined separately, stacked like a sandwich with a filling of pages, and tied together with pretty cord.

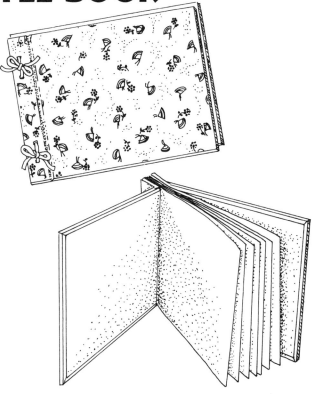

Materials: 2 pieces of single thick Bainbridge board #172 (described further on page 11), each 9 ¼" x 12", for the front and back covers; 2 pieces of good-quality giftwrap paper, each 11 ¼" x 14 ¼", for covering the boards; 2 strips of bond paper, each 9 ¼" x 1 ¾"; 1 package of 9" x 12" construction paper, about 30 sheets, for the lining paper and the pages; 2 pieces of macramé cord or similar cord, each 12" long; paper punch.

1. Cut each board into 2 pieces — 1 piece 9 ¼" x 1 ¼" and the other piece 9 ¼" x 10 ¾".

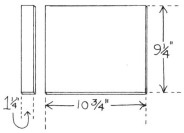

2. Join each pair of pieces together again with a bond paper strip.

Brush slightly diluted glue along 1 short edge of the larger piece of board. Overlap a paper strip ¾" on the glue and smooth it out. Turn the board and strip over and butt them against a ruler. Apply glue to 1 long edge of the narrower piece of board and position it glue-side-down on the bond paper strip, ¼" from the larger board, butted against the ruler. NOTE: Butting the boards against the ruler allows you to keep the boards even and measure ¼" at the same time.

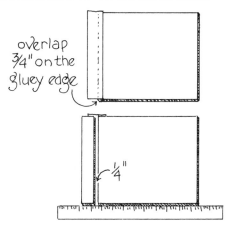

overlap ¾" on the gluey edge

¼"

Repeat this process to join the other pair of pieces. Allow both joined pairs to dry.

3. Cover the boards with the 11¼" x 14¼" covering papers.

Designate 1 pair of joined boards as the front cover and the other pair as the back cover. From now on, they must be treated accordingly, as you will see in the drawings. This is especially important if you are working with a covering paper that has a directional pattern.

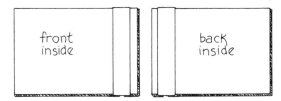

Cover the front with paper first. Lay the paper flat, wrong side up. Center the front cover on it, with the bond paper strip facing up. Outline the cover with pencil, remove it, and clip off the corners of the paper.

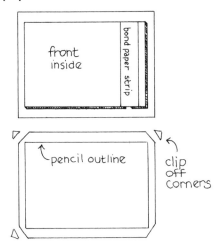

With a large brush, apply slightly diluted glue to the front cover and lay it on the covering paper within the pencil line. Immediately turn the front cover and paper over and smooth the paper out firmly, pushing it slightly into the valley between the joined pieces of board. Turn the cover over to the inside again.

Brush glue on the long edges, bring the paper up, and smooth it over the glue. Brush glue into the paper at the corners of the board and on the short edges. Make neat corners as shown, bring the paper up over the glue and smooth it out. Use a small brush to glue down any loose corners and edges. Bend the front cover out at the joint to set it.

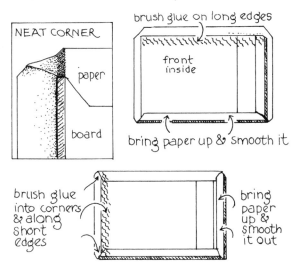

Repeat this process to cover the back.

4. Cut small square holes for the cords to pass through the front and back covers.

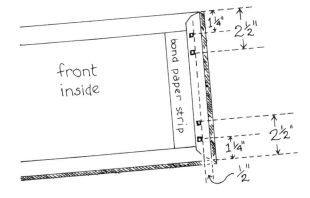

Mark the positions of the 4 holes on the inside of the front cover. Working on a cutting surface, cut out the small squares with a single-edge razor blade and an X-acto knife. Cut each hole by pressing the sharp corner of the razor blade through each side of the marked square. Wiggle and work the blade until it goes all the way through the board; then turn the board over and cut back from the outside to the inside. Use the X-acto knife to help as necessary, especially in the corners of the square holes.

Mark the positions for 4 holes on the inside of the back cover: Stack the front cover on the back cover, perfectly aligned, and mark through the already-cut holes with pencil. Then cut holes in the back cover the same way you cut them in the front cover.

5. Glue the lining papers to the inside of the front and back covers.

From the package of construction paper, pick 2 pieces to be the lining papers; they are exactly the right size as they are. Brush slightly diluted glue over the inside of the front cover, almost to the edges, and center 1 of the lining papers on the glue. Do the same thing on the inside back cover. When the lining papers have dried, use the X-acto knife to cut the square holes in the lining paper, working from the outside of the front cover and the outside of the back cover.

6. Assemble the construction paper for the pages and punch holes for the cords to pass through.

For the pages, pick as many sheets of construction paper as you want, eliminating any colors that don't look good with the covers or the lining papers. Take 1 of the pages and sandwich it between the front and back covers, aligning the page with the lining paper of the back cover and then aligning the front cover with the back cover. With pencil, mark the sandwiched page at each of the 4 square holes.

Take the page out and punch holes at the pencil marks. This page is the pattern for punching holes in all the other pages. Simply stack 3 or 4 pages, align them under the pattern page, and punch the holes. Repeat until all the pages are punched.

7. Stack the parts of the album and tie them together with the cords.

Make a pile of the back cover, the pages, and the front cover, stacking them so that all the holes are aligned. Push the ends of the cords through the holes as shown, tie double knots (and bows if you like), and snip off the excess cord.

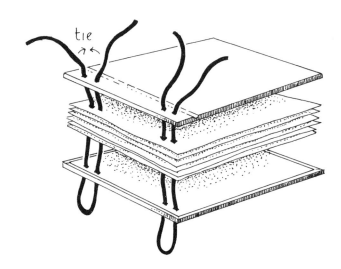

SINGLE-SIGNATURE BOOK

A signature is a group of pages stitched together down a center fold and bound into a book as a unit. Commercial books have many signatures, but binding such a large book would be difficult for the amateur. What we can do instead is make a simple, elegant book with 1 signature.

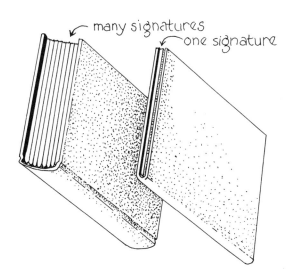

many signatures
one signature

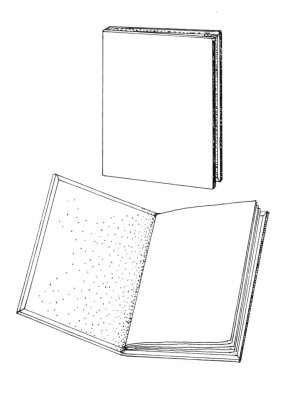

Materials: 2 pieces of single thick Bainbridge board #172, each 8 ½" x 11", for the front and back covers; 1 strip of bond paper, 2" x 11", for joining the boards; 1 piece of medium or heavy weight charcoal paper 13" x 19 ¼" for covering the outside of the boards; 1 piece of light or medium weight charcoal paper 10 7/8" x 17 1/8" for lining the boards; 2 pieces of light or medium weight charcoal paper, each 10 ¾" x 16 ½", for the endpapers; 10 pieces of bond paper, each 10 ¾" x 16 ½", for the pages; medium-size needle and heavy-duty thread that matches the endpapers.

1. Stitch the endpapers and pages together to form the signature.

Each 10 ¾" x 16 ½" sheet of bond and charcoal paper is a double page. Stack the 10 pieces of bond paper on top of the 2 endpapers. Tap them all into alignment and fold them in half. Unfold them, keeping them aligned, and clip with bulldog clips.

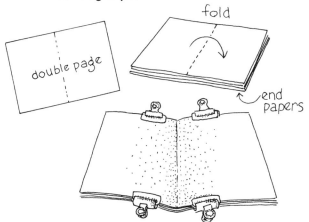

fold

double page

end papers

Make pencil dots along the center fold at 1" intervals; the pages will be stitched together at these dots. Prepare holes for the sewing by pushing the needle through all the pages at each pencil dot. Thread the needle with a 2 yard piece of thread, pulled double, and sew the pages together as shown, keeping the thread taut. Tie the ends of thread together, put a drop of glue on the knot, and cut off any thread in excess of 1". Glue the ends of thread to the back endpaper.

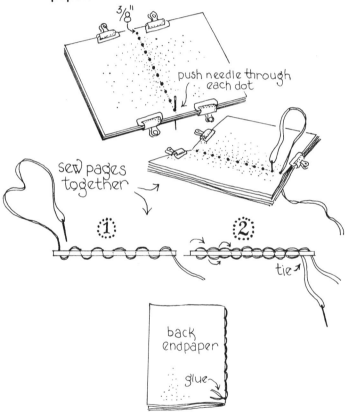

push needle through each dot

sew pages together

① ②

tie

back endpaper

glue

Trim the edges of the pages and set the signature aside for now.

front endpaper

trim pages evenly, using single-edge blade or mat knife

2. Join the front and back boards together with the bond paper strip.

Brush slightly diluted glue on the long edge of the back of 1 board. Overlap the bond paper strip 7/8" on the glue and smooth it out. Turn the board and strip over and butt them against a ruler. Apply glue to 1 long edge of the back of the second board and position it glue-side-down on the paper strip, ¼" from the first board, butting against the ruler. Allow to dry. NOTE: Butting the boards against the ruler keeps the boards even and allows you to measure ¼" at the same time.

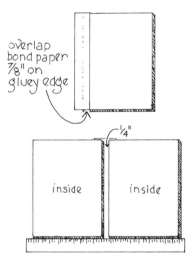

overlap bond paper ⅞" on gluey edge

¼"

inside   inside

3. Cover the joined boards with the 13" x 19 ¼" piece of medium or heavy weight charcoal paper.

Center the joined boards on the charcoal paper, with the back of the boards (the side the strip is glued on) touching the paper. Outline the boards with pencil, remove the boards, and clip off the corners of the charcoal paper.

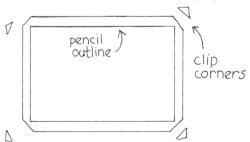

pencil outline

clip corners

With a large brush, apply slightly diluted glue all over the backs of the boards and paper strip. Position the joined boards glue-side-down on the charcoal paper, within the pencil outline. Immediately turn the boards and paper over and smooth the paper firmly and repeatedly, until the paper has adhered all the way to the edges of the boards.

Turn the boards back over and brush glue on the long edges of the boards. Bring the paper up and smooth it firmly over the glue. Be sure to press the paper into the space between the boards — it won't touch the bond paper but it will make a depression.

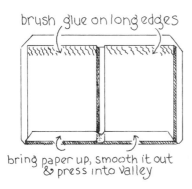

brush glue on long edges

bring paper up, smooth it out & press into valley

Brush glue into the paper at the corners of the boards and along the short edges of the boards. Make neat corners as shown, bring the paper up and smooth it firmly over the glue. Use a small brush to glue down any loose edges and corners. Allow to dry.

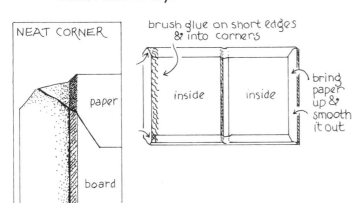

NEAT CORNER

paper

board

brush glue on short edges & into corners

inside   inside

bring paper up & smooth it out

4. Line the covered boards with the 10 7/8" x 17 1/8" piece of light or medium weight charcoal paper.

Center the charcoal paper over the inside of the boards — without glue — to see how it fits. Remove the paper. With a large brush, apply slightly diluted glue to the boards (almost all the way to the edges) and along the valley between them. Center the paper carefully on the boards again, pressing it firmly into the valley to make a depression and smoothing it over the boards. If the lining is oversized or crooked on the edges, trim it carefully with a sharp blade or mat knife, cutting through the paper only. Use a small brush to glue down any loose edges and corners. Wipe away excess glue with a damp (not wet) paper towel. Allow the lining to dry. When it is dry, set the spine by folding up first 1 board and then the other, as shown. Repeat this folding several times.

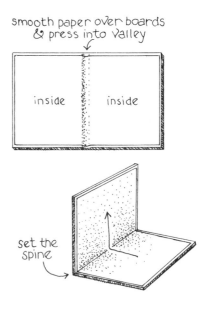

smooth paper over boards & press into valley

inside   inside

set the spine

5. Glue the signature into the cover; the back of the last endpaper of the signature will be glued directly to the inside of the back cover.

Open the cover and put the signature in place on the inside of the back cover to get the feel of the correct positioning. Note that the folded edge of the signature lines up exactly with the edge of the back cover; it should not extend out over the spine. Remove the signature.

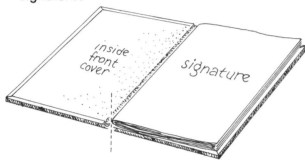

With a large brush, apply slightly diluted glue to the inside of the back cover, almost to the edges. Carefully place the signature in position over the glue, lining up the folded edge of the signature with the edge of the back cover as you did on the practice run. Work quickly. Lift all the pages of the signature except the last page (the endpaper) which is now glued to the inside of the back cover. Wipe away excess glue and smooth the endpaper over the back cover. There will probably be wrinkles and air bubbles. Smooth down the wrinkles as best you can; they will lessen when the paper dries. With a sharp blade, make a small slit in each air bubble and press the air out through the slit.

Fold the pages (but not the front cover) back over the endpaper and press the signature down firmly at the folded edge; hold it so it adheres to the board. Slip several large pieces of scrap paper between the glued-down endpaper and the rest of the pages to absorb moisture and prevent wrinkling. Close the front cover. Stack heavy books on top and allow to set for 15 minutes.

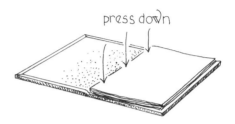

Remove the heavy books and open to the glued-down endpaper. Use a small brush to glue down any loose edges and corners. Wipe away excess glue. Close the book, leaving the scrap papers in place, and press under heavy books overnight.

8. MASKS, TOYS, & SILLY HATS

Like the circus, this chapter is for children of all ages. I had quite a good time inventing it: I made a different hat for every day of the week; I played with miniature houses and trees; I gave finger puppet shows for an audience of one — me. I've had my fun; now it's your turn.

MASKS

Every trick-or-treater knows that when you put on a mask, you turn into an ostrich: You think that with your face hidden, no one will know who you are. It's not true, of course, but go ahead and act silly anyway.

The Basic Masks

A mask can cover your whole face or just your eyes and head. Here are some basic shapes that you can enlarge onto stiff paper and decorate in dozens of ways.

Materials: Stiff paper like 2- or 3-ply Bristol board or poster board; ribbon or heavy yarn.

Draw a 1" graph on the stiff paper. Draw the outline of the basic mask box by box, using the pattern as a guide. Cut out the mask with scissors. The pencilled side of the mask is the wrong side.

Hold the mask over the face of the person who will wear it. If it is too large, remove it and trim it down. Hold it over the person's face again and use pencil to mark the position of the eyes (and nose and mouth if it is a full-face mask). Remove the mask and cut out the eyes (and nose and mouth), checking the position and size after cutting. Punch or cut a hole in each side of the mask. Tie an 18" piece of ribbon or heavy yarn to each hole. These pieces will tie around the masquerader's head to hold the mask in place.

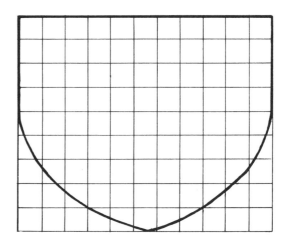

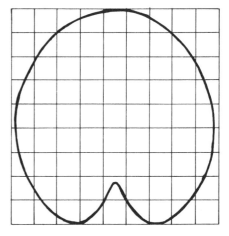

mark

punch holes

cut out

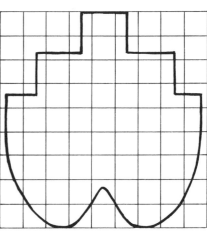

Decorating the Mask

Collect an assortment of decorative materials and go to town making monster faces, animals, and fantasy faces. Think 3-dimensionally when you are decorating; let the trimming stick up, pop off, or dangle down, as well as lie flat. Read all the suggestions before starting. Use undiluted glue for applying the decorations to the mask.

Materials (any of the following): Colored papers of all kinds; bits of yarn, ribbon, and fabric; sequins and spangles; feathers; leaves; bits of trimmings like rickrack, lace, and braid; buttons; beads; beans and seeds; doilies; paper drinking straws; gummed stickers.

Suggestions

1. Paper decorations can be torn, fringed, pinked, scalloped, curled, pleated, or punched with a paper punch.

2. Think of all the parts of a human or animal face: ears, eyebrows, nose, cheeks, chin, eyelashes, hair, moustache, beard, whiskers, mane, horns, antlers. Any of these can be decorations for the mask.

3. Exaggerate: Noses can be long; beards can be curly; ears can be huge. Nothing has to look real.

4. Invent wild combinations of textures, colors, and different papers.

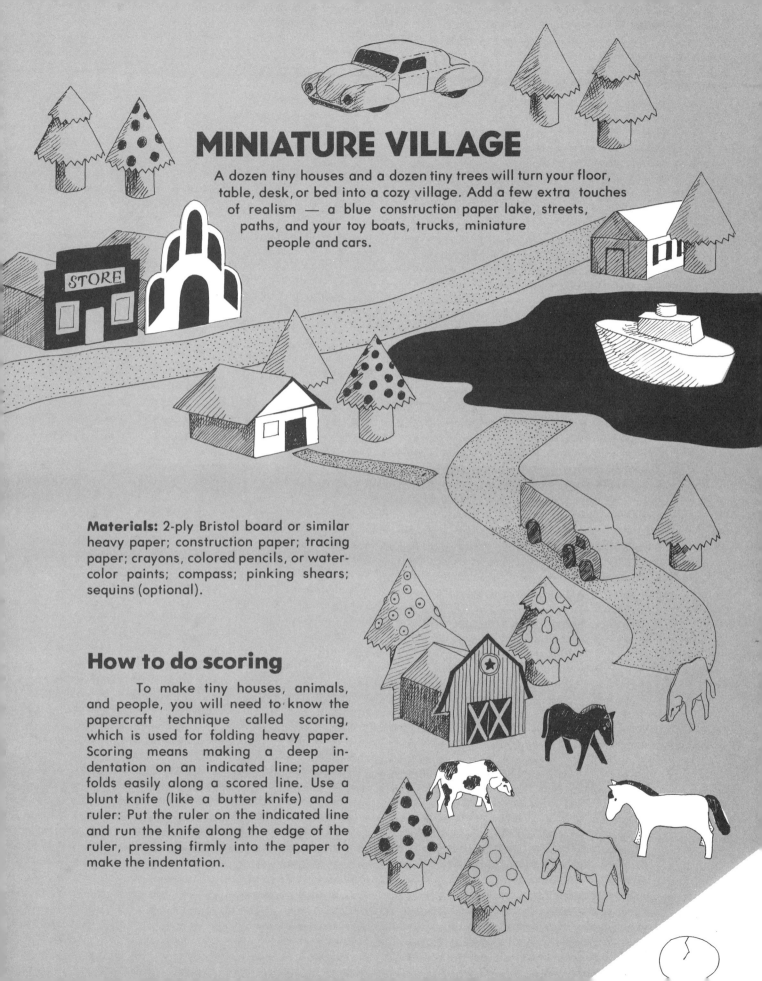

MINIATURE VILLAGE

A dozen tiny houses and a dozen tiny trees will turn your floor, table, desk, or bed into a cozy village. Add a few extra touches of realism — a blue construction paper lake, streets, paths, and your toy boats, trucks, miniature people and cars.

Materials: 2-ply Bristol board or similar heavy paper; construction paper; tracing paper; crayons, colored pencils, or water-color paints; compass; pinking shears; sequins (optional).

How to do scoring

To make tiny houses, animals, and people, you will need to know the papercraft technique called scoring, which is used for folding heavy paper. Scoring means making a deep indentation on an indicated line; paper folds easily along a scored line. Use a blunt knife (like a butter knife) and a ruler: Put the ruler on the indicated line and run the knife along the edge of the ruler, pressing firmly into the paper to make the indentation.

Tiny Houses

Each house is made in the same way. Draw a 6" square on Bristol board and pencil it into sixteenths. Cut out the square. Cut and score on the lines as indicated. Fold on the scored lines to set the shape. Unfold. Decorate with crayons, colored pencils, paints, or construction paper cut-outs.

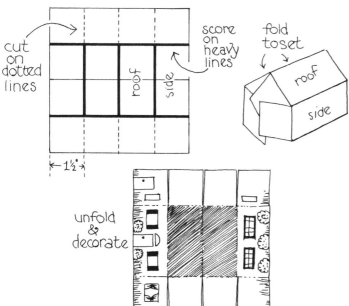

Refold the square into a house and glue the sides into position. The slope of the roof can be steep or shallow. Clip the sides with clothespins or paper clips while the glue dries.

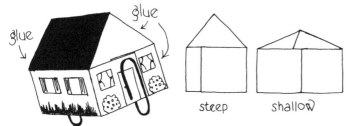

Suggestions

1. For a larger or smaller house than the size given, make the square larger or smaller.

2. Decorate the house with a glued-on construction paper roof. Let it overhang the house a little bit on all sides.

3. Make a Hollywood-style false front for 1 end of the house. Cut it from construction paper and decorate it with windows and a door.

Tiny Trees

Each tree is made the same way. For the trunk of the tree, cut a piece of construction paper 3" x 4". Roll it into a cylinder and glue. With a compass, draw a circle 6" in diameter on construction paper. Cut it out with pinking shears. Cut the circle in half. Roll 1 half into a cone and glue. (Use the other half-circle for another tree.) Dab glue around the top edge of the trunk and set the cone on it. Allow the glue to dry.

Suggestions

1. For a larger tree, start with a larger cone and cylinder.
2. Top the tree with another smaller cone made from slightly more than 1 half of the circle 3" in diameter.
3. Decorate the tree with sequins or construction paper fruit.

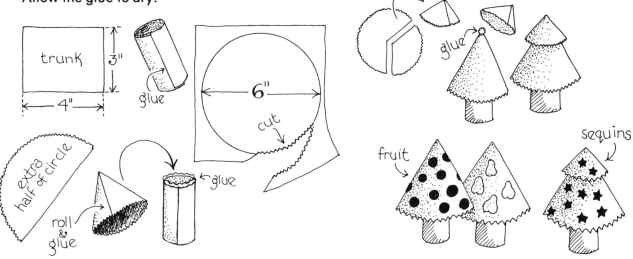

Tiny Animals

Make a pattern by tracing the animal on tracing paper and cutting it out. For each animal draw around the pattern twice on construction or bond paper, and cut out on the outlines. Glue the 2 cut-outs together along the top edge to make a 4-legged animal. When the glue is dry, decorate with crayons, paints, or pencils. Bend the body and legs out so the animal will stand.

FLIPBOOK

A flipbook is something like a movie. It is a little book with a picture on each page; each picture is a little bit different from the one before. When you flip through all the pages, the picture seems to be moving. If you flip through the corners of <u>this</u> book, pages 97 through 127, you will see how a flipbook works. Here's how to make one.

Materials: 4 sheets of typing paper, each 8 ½ " x 11"; colored pencils.

Cut each sheet of paper into 8 parts as shown. You will have 32 pieces of paper. Glue the pieces together — 1 at a time — at 1 short end. Be sure to keep the pages carefully lined up as you glue each piece to the one before.

Now you can draw the pictures. Think about what the flipbook will show before you start drawing. It doesn't have to tell a story, but something has to happen little by little. For example, you could draw a small shape and have it get bigger and bigger until it fills the page. Or you could draw a face and have it smile wider and wider while a beard grows longer and longer.

Make the first drawing on the bottom page, working only on the lower half of the page. When the first drawing is done, cover it with the blank page above. If you look carefully, you can see the first drawing through the blank page. This is very important because the second drawing is based on the first, although it should be slightly different. When the second drawing is done, cover it with the next blank page and do the next drawing. Continue drawing on each page, making each drawing a little different from the one before, until you reach the top of the pile. Flip through the book from bottom to top and top to bottom to see the picture move.

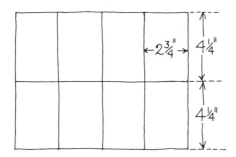

PUPPETS

Simple Puppet

Cut a rectangle of bond or construction paper 3" wide and as high as the puppeteer's finger. Decorate the center section of the rectangle with a face, clothes, hair, etc., using paint, crayons, or felt-tip markers. Roll the paper into a cylinder that fits loosely on the finger (trim it if it is too long) and glue or tape it closed.

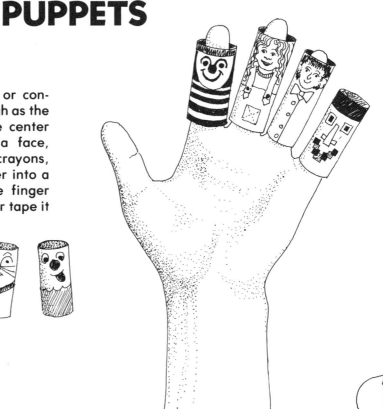

Puppet with Finger-Legs

Make this puppet from heavy paper or thin board — 3- or 4-ply Bristol board, poster board, or shirt cardboard. First trace the pattern onto tracing paper and cut it out. Use this pattern as a general guide: Outline the pattern on heavy paper and before cutting it out draw your own additions (hat, ears, crazy hair) or corrections (change the arm positions, draw a different head shape). Cut out the puppet and the holes and try it on to be sure the finger-holes are large enough. Enlarge the holes if necessary. Decorate the puppet with paints, crayons, or felt-tip markers, or with paper cut-outs.

doily

doily

pipe cleaner

yarn

giftwrap

Puppet-on-a-Stick

For each puppet, you will need a thin dowel; stiff paper (3- or 4-ply Bristol board, poster board, or shirt cardboard); construction paper; a few crayons; Scotch or masking tape; and decorative materials like sequins, feathers, pompons from ball fringe, bits of ribbon and cloth, and scraps of colored paper.

Cut a simple body and head from the stiff paper. Make caterpillar arms and legs (see drawings) and attach them to the body as shown. Glue on construction paper hands and feet. Use decorative materials and crayons to jazz up the puppet — add a hat, ears, moustache, buttons, or anything you like. Glue <u>and</u> tape the body to the dowel.

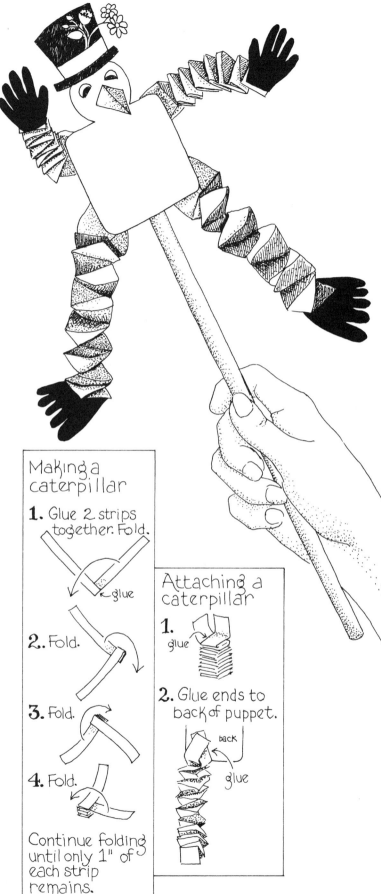

Making a caterpillar

1. Glue 2 strips together. Fold.

2. Fold.

3. Fold.

4. Fold.

Continue folding until only 1" of each strip remains.

Attaching a caterpillar

1. glue

2. Glue ends to back of puppet.

back

glue

1st hat

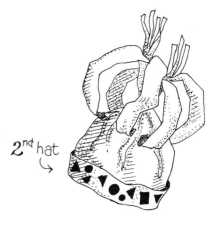

2nd hat

SILLY HATS

Crepe Paper Hats

Materials: 1 folded roll of crepe paper plus some scraps of other colors; 6" pieces of yarn or string; tape measure.

These hats are made in basically the same way, with slight variations on the tops. First measure your head with the tape measure. Unfold the roll of crepe paper and cut off a piece as wide as that measurement, keeping the full height of the paper. Overlap 1 end of the paper 1" on the other end and glue to form a tube. Turn up the lower edge to make a cuff. Put the tube on your head and gather it with your hand. Take it off and tie it with yarn or string, wrapping the string around several times and double knotting it. Decorate the cuff with scraps of other colors.

Cut the top section into strips about 1 ½" wide but do not cut down as far as the string. For the first hat, cut fringes in half of the strips and then muss them to separate the strips. For the second hat, bend almost all the strips around and glue them to the main part of the hat; leave a few strips standing up but clip them shorter and fringe them.

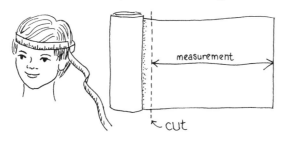

measurement

cut

overlap & glue

gather   tie

cuff

Flower Hat

Materials: Roll of shelf paper; scraps of colored papers; spangles; tape measure.

Measure your head. Cut a piece of shelf paper 10" wide and as long as the head measurement plus 1". Fold in half the long way and cut scallops in the unfolded edge. Slip 1 end of the band into the other for 1" and glue. Cut narrow strips of colored paper and glue a short fringe of "hair" around the front. Glue longer strips around the sides and curl each strip over a pencil. Cut out simple flowers, curl the petals, and glue a spangle to the center of each. Glue each flower to the hat.

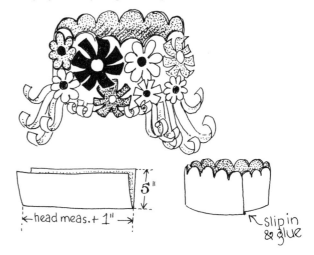

5"

head meas. + 1"

slip in & glue

Petal Hat

Materials: Roll of shelf paper; folded roll of crepe paper; scraps of colored papers; tape measure.

Measure your head with the tape measure. Cut a piece of shelf paper 7" wide and as long as the head measurement plus 1". Fold in half the long way, slip 1 end inside the other for 1", and glue. Unroll the crepe paper and cut 6 petals as shown. Dab glue on the straight edge of each petal and pinch-pleat it. Glue each pinch-pleated petal between the inner surfaces of the band: Put glue on both surfaces and sandwich the petal between them; press the insides together so they stick to each other, too. Decorate the band.

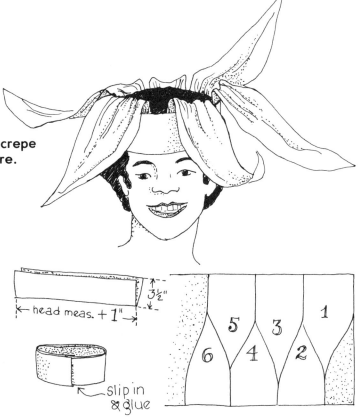

Folded Hat

Make this hat from a piece of paper 18" square for a small head, 20" square for a medium, and 24" square for a large.

1. Fold in half.

2. Fold points down.

3. Fold points up.

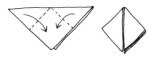

4. Fold points out.

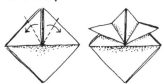

5. Fold point up.

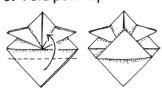

6. Fold narrow strip up.

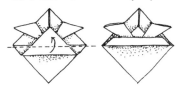

7. Turn hat over. Fold point up.

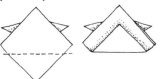

8. Fold narrow strip up.

9. Turn hat over and open it up to wear it.

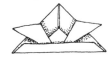

9. BOXES & BASKETS

Boxes and baskets are first cousins once removed. It's true that you put things in both of them, but the family resemblance ends there. Take advantage of the differences: Boxes are sturdy, useful containers; baskets are frivolous decorations for parties and holidays.

How to do scoring

To make the Bristol board boxes and the baskets in this chapter, you will need to know about the papercraft technique called scoring, which is used when you want to fold a paper or board. Scoring means making a deep indentation or a shallow cut (just breaking the surface but not cutting through) along an indicated line. The paper or board then folds easily along the scored line. Use a blunt knife for making an indentation; use a mat knife, X-acto knife, or single-edge razor blade for making a shallow cut.

BRISTOL BOARD BOXES

These simple boxes make lovely caddies for the odds and ends on your bureau and desk, for holding cuff links, earrings, paper clips, rubber bands, loose change, and other small things. They are just right for packaging small presents, too.

To make the boxes, you will need 4-ply Bristol board and undiluted glue, as well as a ruler, metal straight edge, plenty of single-edge razor blades or a mat knife and blades, clips, right-angle triangle, compass, and a cutting surface. (Further information about materials can be found in the first chapter of the book.)

Square Box with Fitted Cover

Draw the shapes for the box and the cover on 4-ply Bristol board, measuring carefully, using the patterns as guides. Note that the cover is slightly larger than the box. Cut out each shape with a mat knife or single-edge blade and a metal straight edge. Score the heavy lines as indicated, using a blade (not a blunt knife). Fold on the scored lines. Glue the tabs inside the box and inside the cover and clip while the glue is drying. When the glue is dry, remove the clips. Decorate the box if you like, using the drawings for ideas.

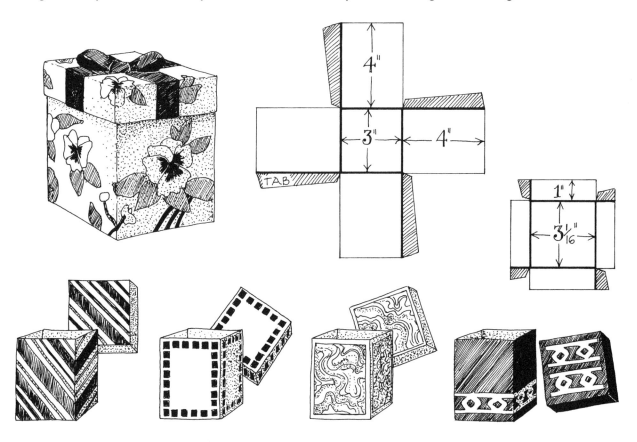

Trinket Box with Fitted Cover

The instructions for making this 6-sided box and cover are the same as the instructions for the square box, except that drawing the shape requires more measuring.

Use a compass to draw a circle with a radius of 2" (diameter of 4"). Keeping the compass at the same 2" setting, mark off 6 points on the circle: Put the point of the compass on the circle at any spot and swing the pencil end of the compass to make a little mark that intersects the circle; pick up the compass, move the point to the pencil mark, and swing the pencil end again to make another mark on the circle; continue doing this until you have worked all the way around the circle, dividing it into 6 parts. Connect the 6 points on the circle with straight lines. Erase the circle, leaving the hexagon. Draw the sides (tall or short) and tabs of the box as shown. The solid lines in the drawing are the actual lines you must draw; the dotted lines are the connections between the lines. You need not draw the dotted lines or else you may draw them and then erase them.

The cover of the box is drawn in an identical manner but note that the compass setting is slightly larger, 2 1/16". Cut out each shape with a mat knife or single-edge blades and a metal straight edge. Score the heavy lines as indicated, using a blade (not a blunt knife). Fold on the scored lines. Glue the tabs inside the box and inside the cover and clip while the glue is drying. Remove the clips when the glue is dry. The drawings show ideas for decorating the box.

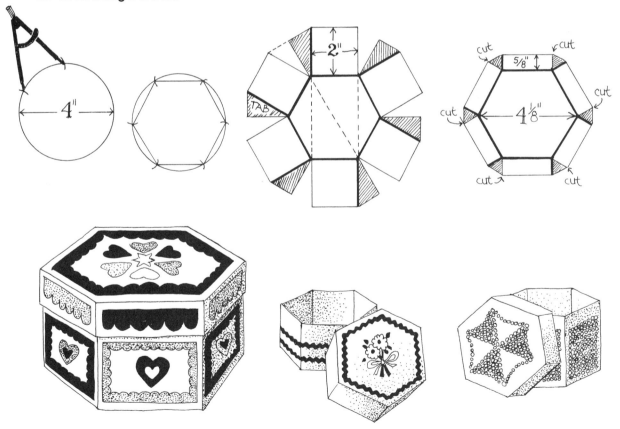

Wraparound Box

The wraparound box is made of a rectangular frame glued into a wraparound cover. In addition to the materials previously mentioned for making Bristol board boxes, you will need 2 pieces of thin string or crochet cotton (pearl cotton or Knit-Cro-Sheen, available at the 5-and-10, each 1 yard long. You will also need a gummed sticker or small paper cut-out.

Draw the narrow strip with tabs — the frame — and the wide strip (no tabs) — the cover — on 4-ply Bristol board, using the patterns as guides. Cut out each shape with mat knife or single-edge blades and metal straight edge. Score the heavy lines as indicated, using a blade (not a blunt knife), and fold on the scored lines.

Glue the tab at the end of the narrow strip inside the opposite end. Overlap and glue the other 4 tabs at their corners, keeping the tabs perpendicular to the sides of the box and keeping the sides of the box at right angles to each other. Maintaining all these right angles ensures that the frame will lie flat and perfectly rectangular when it is glued inside the wraparound cover.

Apply glue to the underside of the tabs and center the frame on the bottom of the wraparound cover. Hold it firmly in place until the glue dries. Glue the 2 pieces of string to the top of the wraparound cover. When the glue is dry, cover the spot with the gummed sticker or paper cut-out. Tie the box up and cut off any excess string.

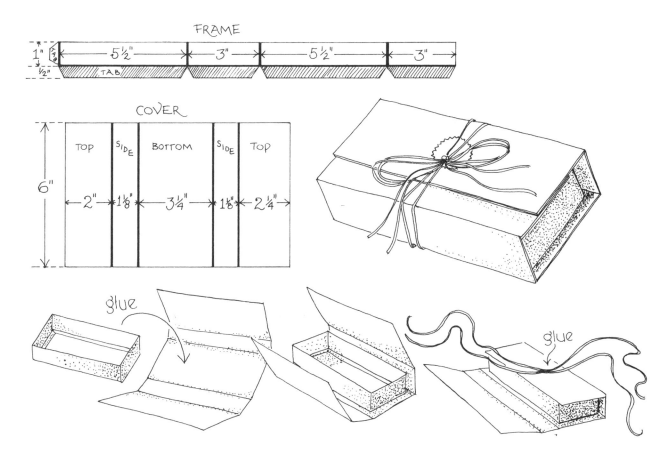

BASKETS

Paper baskets are purely decorative. They are delightful for party tables (filled with nuts and candy), centerpieces (filled with paper flowers or dried flowers), May Day (filled with fresh flowers and a little present) or Easter (filled with cellophane grass and chocolate eggs).

Simple Basket

Materials: Construction paper or other firm colored paper; compass; blunt knife for scoring.

Draw a circle with a 4 ¼ " radius (8 ½ " diameter). The entire circle is used to make the basket. Draw the measurements of the basket within the circle. Cut out the circle with scissors and then snip and score as indicated. Fold on the scored lines. Glue the tabs to the <u>outside</u> of the basket. Glue on a handle and decorate the basket if you like.

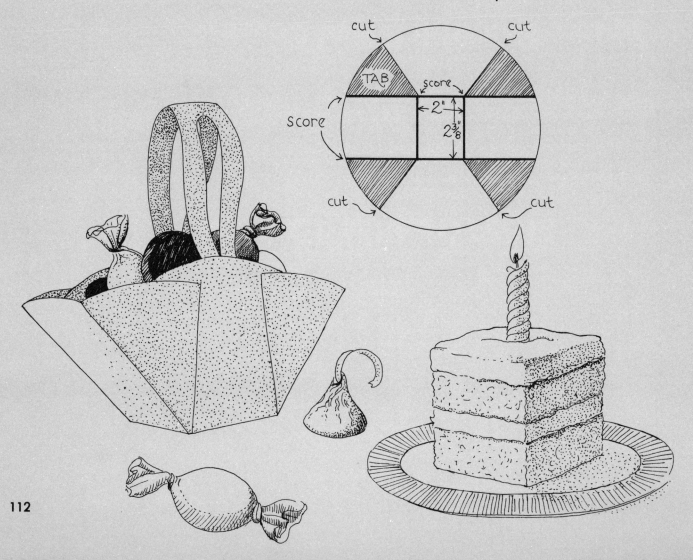

Two-Pocket Basket

Materials: Construction paper or other firm colored paper; 45°-90°-45° triangle; blunt knife for scoring.

The basket is made of 2 identical pockets that are glued together in the middle. Draw the pocket shape twice, using the pattern as a guide, and cut out the shapes. Score each shape as indicated, using the blunt knife, and fold on the scored lines. Glue the tabs to the inside of each pocket.

Make ½" snips in the untabbed rectangular side of each pocket. Fold down as shown to make tabs. Glue the 2 pockets together by overlapping these tabs: Glue 1 tab to the <u>inside</u> of the other pocket; glue the other tab to the <u>outside</u> of the first pocket. Glue the pockets together on the sides as shown.

Fold the 4 triangular sides of the basket out at the centers. Glue a handle to the basket.

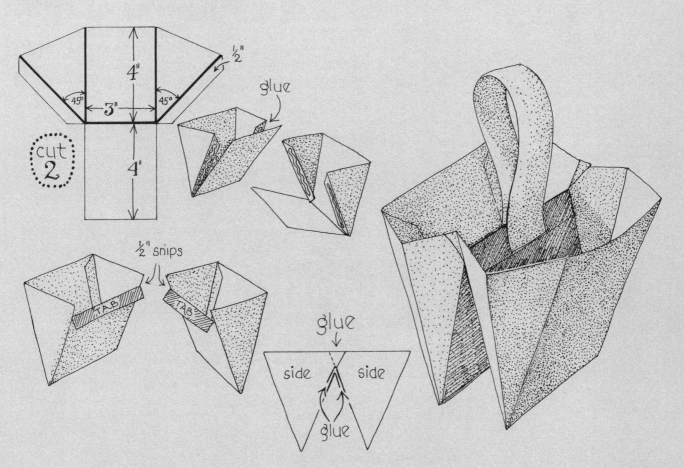

Flower Basket

Materials: 9" x 12" construction paper or other firm colored paper; 30°-60°-90° triangle; compass; blunt knife for scoring; decorative materials like doilies, ribbon, and gummed flower stickers.

Measure and draw the basket shape carefully, using the pattern as a guide. Note that the curved edges are drawn using a compass and the span of the curved section is determined by measuring with the 60° angle of the triangle.

Use the scissors to cut out the shape. Score on the heavy lines as indicated, using a blunt knife, and fold on the scored lines. Note that 2 of the lines fold <u>out</u> while the others fold in. Glue the tabs to the inside of the basket.

Glue handles to the basket and decorate.

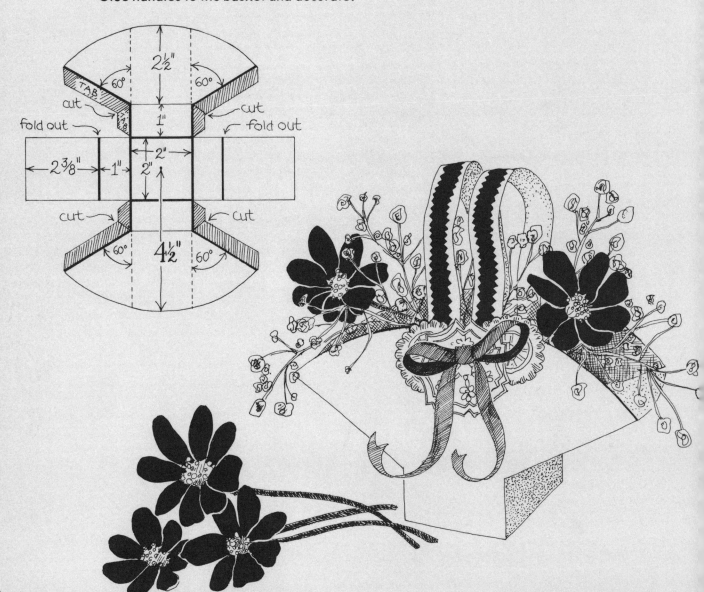

Woven Basket

Materials: Assorted colors of construction paper or other firm colored paper; compass.

First make the bottom of the basket. Open the compass to a width of 1 7/8" and draw a circle on construction paper. Increase the compass opening to 2 3/8" and draw a circle concentric with the first circle. Cut out on the outline of the larger circle and then snip tabs every ¼" or so, cutting to the pencil line of the smaller circle. Fold the tabs up. Cut a strip of paper ½" x 12". Dab glue on the outside of the tabs and wrap the strip around them, pressing the tabs to the strip. Overlap and glue the ends of the strip. Set the bottom aside for now.

Cut a piece of paper 3" x 12". Make 5 lengthwise slits, ½" apart, stopping ½" short of each end of the piece. Cut 21 strips of paper, each ½" x 3", in an assortment of colors; cut 1 more strip ¼" x 3". Weave all 22 strips into the longer strips of paper, as shown, using an under-over pattern. Keep the short strips pushed close together. When all 22 strips have been woven, glue the ends of the short strips to the long strips at top and bottom.

Dab glue on the tabs inside the bottom of the basket. Form the woven part of the basket into a cylinder and set it into the bottom, enlarging the cylinder to make it fit snugly. Glue the overlapping ends of the cylinder together. Cut 2 strips of paper for handles and glue them inside the basket as shown.

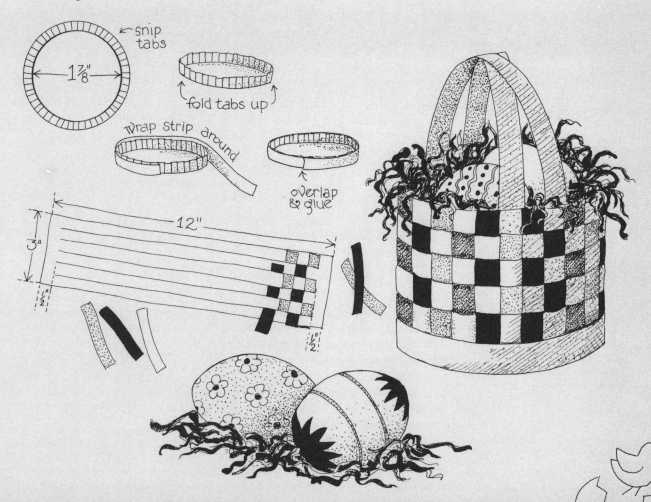

ORIGAMI BOXES

Place a few origami boxes on the dinner table and fill them with mints and salted nuts. When everyone asks where you got those irresistible boxes, take out a square of paper and show them. Make each box from a 7" square of origami paper, flint paper, or giftwrap.

Square Box with Flaps

1. Fold diagonally, crease, and unfold.

2. Fold and crease (points don't reach quite to center). Unfold.

3. Fold each point to the crease, then fold again by rolling over until the folds meet at the center.

4. Fold back in half.

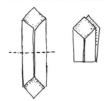

5. Crease and unfold.

6. Bring the center edges down to meet the lower edge. Crease across the back, bringing the point down.

Figure looks like this.

7. Turn over and repeat step 6 on the other side. Now the figure looks like this.

8. Fold side points to center and crease. Fold bottom point up. Fold bottom up again.

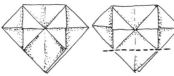

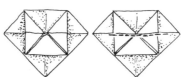

Figure looks like this.

9. Turn over and repeat step 8 on the other side.

Figure looks like this.

10. Rotate the figure and open it up flat. Pull the top flaps to open the box. Straighten out the sides.

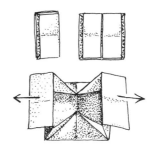

Fancy Box with Points

1. Fold in half and in quarters.

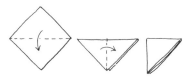

2. Open out the top corner, flatten, and crease.

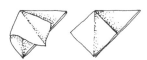

3. Turn over and repeat step 2 on the other side.

4. Fold sides to center and crease.

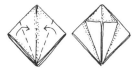

5. Fold, crease, and unfold. Open corners out.

6. Turn over and repeat steps 4 and 5 on the other side.

7. Fold the left side over the right side.

8. Turn over and repeat step 7 on the other side.

9. Fold sides to center.

10. Fold top point up once and then fold the lower edge up again.

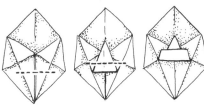

11. Turn over and repeat steps 9 and 10 on the other side.

Figure looks like this now.

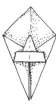

12. Fold left side over right and repeat the folding technique for the top point.

Figure looks like this now.

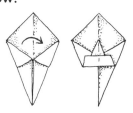

13. Turn over. Fold left side over right. Fold the point up as in previous steps.

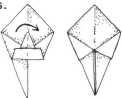

Figure looks like this. Turn figure around.

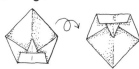

14. Carefully push the sides out. Flatten the bottom.

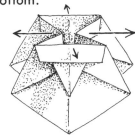

10. NOTES, CARDS, & INVITATIONS

Once I gave a party and sent out store-bought invitations that pictured on the front a small and slightly groggy mermaid draped inside and over the rim of a large champagne glass. The saying under the picture read "Come to an Orgy." This was in 1959, I was 13 years old, and I hadn't the faintest idea what an orgy was. I didn't even know how to pronounce it. The invitations just seemed terribly grown-up and so I sent them.

Naturally, everyone came to that party; they wanted to find out what an orgy was. They didn't make the discovery any sooner than I did, which was when I looked it up in the dictionary several years later. I have had a healthy respect for appropriate cards and invitations ever since.

FOLDED NOTES WITH CUT-PAPER DECORATIONS

Any pretty folded note can be sent as a thank you note, greeting card, invitation, gift enclosure, R.S.V.P., or even a short letter.

Buy a set of perfectly plain folded notes with matching envelopes (available at the 5-and-10 or the stationery store). Decorate a dozen at a clip. Glue single-fold designs — backed with colored papers, if you like — to the front of the notes and write the message inside.

Polish paper-cutting
(pages 30-32)

MOSAIC PATTERN NOTES

Cut construction paper of assorted colors into ½" squares. Glue squares in a design on the front of a store-bought folded note or a folded note you make yourself from a piece of construction paper.

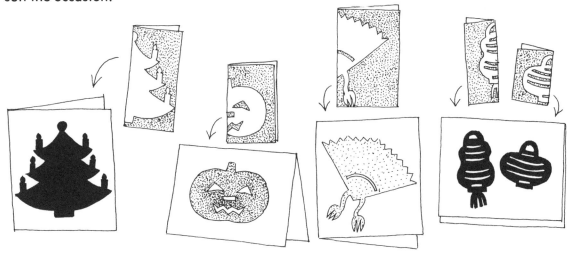

If you know you will be using the notes for special events, you can cut the design to suit the occasion.

PATCHWORK PATTERN NOTES

These designs, based on traditional American patchwork quilt patterns, are pieced together with glue instead of needle and thread. Start with squares, cut the squares into pieces, and arrange the pieces in a geometric pattern. Glue patchwork patterns on folded notes that have matching envelopes, on sheets of plain stationery folded in half, or on pieces of colored paper folded in half. If you use colored paper, make matching or contrasting envelopes to fit (see page 126).

Paper patchwork begins with 1" squares cut from almost any kind of paper — construction paper, Aurora paper, flint paper, giftwrap, or a combination of any of these. Try mixing solid colors and patterns. Cut several dozen squares at a time.

The next step (whether you are following my design or inventing one of your own) is to reserve the whole squares you need and cut other squares into the required triangles, bars, or smaller squares. Arrange the pieces on the folded paper in the correct pattern, first marking the paper with light pencil lines if necessary. Using slightly diluted glue and a small brush, apply glue to the back of each piece and put it back in position.

DECORATED CARDS

Make special-occasion cards or invitations from squares or rectangles of 3- or 4-ply Bristol board. The card is <u>not</u> folded, but it is decorated on the front, with space left for writing a message. Cut the Bristol board to fit a ready-made envelope or plan to make an envelope to fit the card (see page 126).

Framed Card

Decorate the front of the card with a cut-paper frame made in the single-fold method. Apply slightly diluted glue sparingly but completely to the back of the frame and press the frame carefully in position on the board.

Tied-Up Card

Cut a piece of colored paper smaller than the board. Tie it to the board with ribbon or cord slipped into holes punched through both the board and the overlaid paper. Decorate the paper and board with small cut-outs. Write a message on the colored paper.

punch holes

Doily Card

Make a cut-paper doily in the double- or triple-fold method, making sure the doily fits on the board and has either a cut-out blank space or a section of uncut paper in the center for writing the message. Glue the doily to the Bristol board, using slightly diluted glue and a small brush. (Additional ideas for double- and triple-fold cutting can be found on pages 34, 35, 36, and 37).

KNOT NOTES

Write the message inside the paper, fold into either kind of knot as shown, and slip the knot into an envelope for mailing. These notes make unusual invitations.

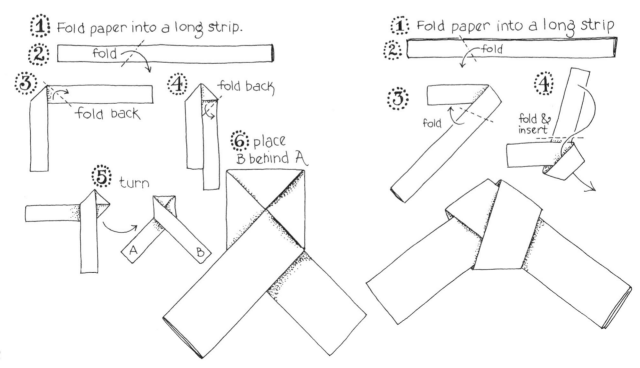

1. Fold paper into a long strip.
2. fold
3. fold back
4. fold back
5. turn
   A   B
6. place B behind A

1. Fold paper into a long strip
2. fold
3. fold
4. fold & insert

FOLDED FIGURE CARDS

A plane, train, tree, cat, fish, fan, teacup, or birthday cake — draw any one of these on a folded sheet of construction paper. Cut it out, decorate it, and you have the perfect, simple greeting card or invitation. Children are whizzes at this and will probably have a dozen terrific ideas to try out. My favorite is the folded hand that you make by outlining your own hand, but the bunch of grapes (for a cocktail party invitation) is running a close second. Write the message or the details of the invitation on the inside of the folded card and send it off in a ready-made envelope.

VALENTINES

For me, Valentine's Day is an all-out excuse for giving in to the desire for excessive hearts, ribbons, and lacy bits of doilies. If you have the same inclination, indulge yourself in all sorts of red and pink papers, gummed heart stickers, gold, silver, and white doilies of various sizes, and plenty of pretty ribbon. Make a different valentine for each friend, using my designs and inventing some of your own. Remember that these valentines are odd shapes, so plan to make matching envelopes (see page 126) or buy sturdy manila envelopes that the valentines will fit in.

Dangling Hearts Valentine

Cut a 3 ¾ " x 4" piece of red paper (construction, flint, Aurora, etc.). Glue parts of doilies around the edge on the back of the paper to make a lacy border. Glue the lace-edged paper to a 4 ½ " x 5" piece of red poster board. Cut 3 hearts out of colored paper and punch a hole in each. Write a message on each heart.
Attach a short piece of colored string or crochet cotton to each heart and glue the ends to the paper. Glue a ribbon bow over the ends of string.

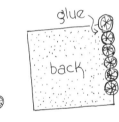

Lace Border Valentine

Cut the outer border of lace from a doily, keeping the border intact. Outline it on a piece of colored paper and cut the paper on the outline. Glue the lace border to the paper, using a small brush and slightly diluted glue. Decorate the lace border with cut-out hearts (red flint paper is nice for this) or gummed heart stickers and write a loving message in the center of the paper.

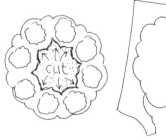

Heart-to-Heart Valentine

Fold a square of red paper in half and then in quarters. Draw a heart pattern as shown and cut away the shaded areas. Unfold the connected hearts and glue them to a backing circle of contrasting paper, perhaps metallic paper, patterned paper, or giftwrap. Write the message on the hearts.

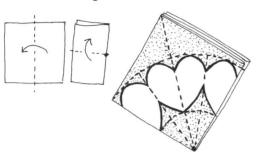

Mosaic Heart

This folded heart is decorated with a tissue paper mosaic in candy colors: light and dark pink, turquoise, yellow, light and dark green, pale blue, lavender, orange, and red for the border.

Cut a heart pattern and outline it on a folded sheet of white paper (construction, 1- or 2-ply Bristol, or bond). The top of the heart pattern should be lined up with the fold. Cut out the heart on the pencil line, leaving the folds intact at the top. Tear a dozen small pieces of each color of tissue; tear more pieces as you need them. Reserve all the red pieces for the border.

Slip a piece of scrap paper between the folded hearts. Cover the top heart completely with pieces of tissue glued down with a small brush and slightly diluted glue. Overlap the pieces slightly, putting different colors next to each other. Glue on a border of red pieces.

Remove the scrap paper and allow the mosaic to dry. Trim the excess tissue from around the edge. The paper will be rippled and uneven; stack heavy books on the card to flatten it. Write the message inside.

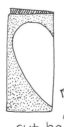

cut heart pattern

outline on folded paper

folds intact

scrap paper

ENVELOPES

To give you an idea of the possibilities, the drawings below show several different styles of custom-made envelopes, each constructed in basically the same way.

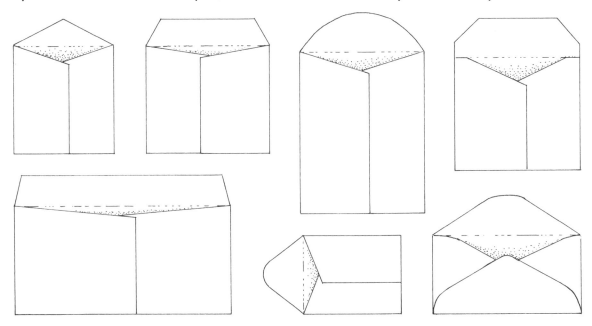

Determine the size the envelope should be. Measure the height and width of the card, note, or invitation and add ½″ to each measurement; this gives you the dimensions of the center part of the envelope. The sides, top, and bottom of the envelope must be large enough to overlap when folded. For example, if the card measures 4″ x 5″, the center section must be 4 ½″ x 5 ½″ and the sides, top, and bottom may be any of the dimensions shown.

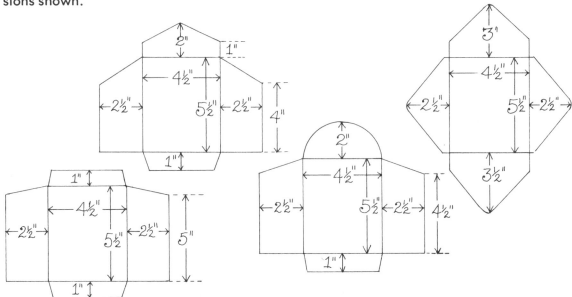

Make each envelope from a single piece of paper. Draw it on the paper with pencil, measuring carefully, and cut it out. Fold the sides and bottom on the pencil lines and glue them together, using slightly diluted glue and a small brush. Make sure that any excess glue has been wiped away, to avoid having the front accidentally glue itself to the back. Allow the envelope to dry completely. Slip the card into the envelope, fold the top down on the pencil line, and glue the envelope shut.

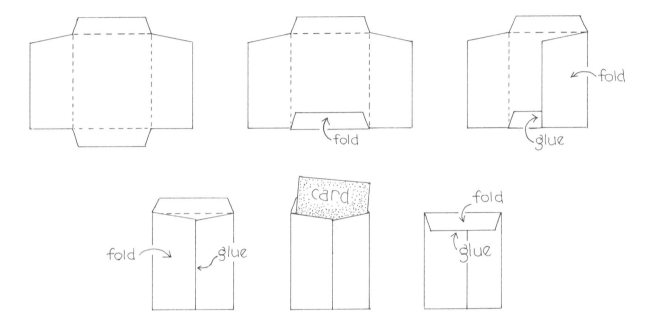